D1028717

THANKS FOR THE POEMS:
A commemorative collection

Edited by

Mary Abbott
Sally Bates
Nika Nordbrock

Published by

Sharlot Hall
MUSEUM
An Arizona History Adventure

Artists and writers
hold personal copyrights on contents.

Front Cover artwork by
George Molnar, Prescott, Arizona

Back Cover artwork by
Joe Beeler, Sedona, Arizona

Book is copyrighted by Sharlot Hall Museum,
Prescott, Arizona 2006
All rights reserved
ISBN # 978-0-927579-23-0

Typesetting and layout work done by
Arizona Cowboy Connection
Chino Valley, Arizona 2006

Printed by Morris Publishing
Kearney, Nebraska

Preface

The Sharlot Hall Museum Press is proud to publish *Thanks for the Poems: A Commemorative Collection*, the latest in a long, diverse, and distinguished line of Sharlot Hall Museum Press publications.

The Sharlot Hall Museum Press can trace its beginnings to 1928 when Sharlot Hall published *The Arizona Rough Rider Monument and Captain W.O. O'Neill*—the first of The Old Capitol Booklets. Introducing the series, Sharlot wrote, "This booklet is the first of a series which will be issued from time to time to be sold for the restoration and upkeep of the Old Governor's Mansion, often called The Old Capitol."

Continuing her introduction, Sharlot promised, "These booklets will each contain the history and romance of some locality, city, town, mining camp, or other point of interest in Yavapai County."

In subsequent years, the Museum Press has published books by Sharlot such as *Cactus and Pine* and *Poems of a Ranch Woman*, as well as ones about her such as *Sharlot Herself* by Nancy Kirkpatrick Wright. Other Press titles include *Ernest W. McFarland Biography, Meeting the 4 O'Clock Train, Coexisting with Urban Wildlife,* and *Chinese Sojourners in Territorial Arizona*.

As for purchasing Sharlot Hall Museum Press titles, you can obtain them through the Museum Store located on the first floor of the historic Bashford House at the corner of Gurley and McCormick Streets, by calling 928.445.3122, or on the Museum's website. **www.sharlot.org.**

THANKS TO OUR BOOK SPONSORS

Rex & Ruth Maughan
Maughan Ranches, Kirkland, Arizona

T K Bar	East Fork
Diamond Two	West Fork
Hozoni	Desert Hills
Z Triangle	Bow Nine
P Bar	Buck Horn
Cross S	Fort Rock
El Oso	Zane Grey
North Fork	

Steve & Joan Pierce
Las Vegas Ranch, Prescott, Arizona

Sharlot Hall Museum

The logo was designed by Dave Holl in 1990 especially for the Arizona Cowboy Poets Gathering.

Thanks . . .
for the poems!

This book is dedicated to our poetic friends who have traveled far and near to share with us their poetry, songs, and above that their hearts: to those who were willing to set their feelings and thoughts on paper and above that to share with others, to all those volunteers who gave of their time and energy and above that their heartfelt support, to those who have gone on before us to pave the way and above that paved the way for a younger generation who will continue to share and love cowboy poetry.
<u>*Thanks for the poems!!*</u>

1991 Poster Artwork   By Shawn Cameron

FOREWORD

When the poetry submissions started arriving, we weren't a bit surprised at the quality and quantity from our fellow-poets. It was exciting to see what kind of response we'd get, being pretty sure our "family" of cowboy poets would provide all we needed to get the job done. They always have! And, sure enough, they did it again.

Within the pages of this book are poems each person selected from their "stash" of heart-felt writings. But the ones we treasure the most are those sent by the family members of our poets who've left this range and headed for higher pastures. In the past twenty years of cowboy poetry gatherings, something really wonderful has happened: the weaving together of a fabric of men and women who have become a family. We miss those who have gone before us, and are so glad their own families allowed us to include something from their hands in this collection.

It is our hope that you'll read these pages with the same heart-felt memories they have given us. That each time you read a poem, you'll think of the person who wrote it, and how important they have become in your circle of friends and family. That, as you read the words, you'll remember their faces and think fondly of them and the time you've spent together. That you will find truth and substance in the writings of these men and women who forage for the words to send forth a message of the inner workings of a culture which must not fade from our hearts.

It's been twenty years' worth of valuable time and energy from every person involved in the Gathering, from poets to volunteers.

It seems like only yesterday . . .

THE SOURCE

Joel Nelson

The stories may spring from a boxcar camp
Sitting out by some Aermotor mill
Taking form in the glow of a kerosene lamp
As the icy wind lays and grows still

Or the poem may evolve on the saddlehouse bench
While the saddlehouse cat purrs nearby
And a piece of a feedsack will do in a pinch
Stationery from Rancher's supply.

The verse could be penned from a high rise suite
Written down without pretense or hoax
And be treasured through time for the rhyme and the beat
And integrity that it evokes.

But whatever the source of the piece we inspect
Be it villa or bunkhouse cot
The ones of the "clan" will be quick to detect
If the author has "been there" or not!

INTRODUCTION

During the summers of 1983 and 1984, Joe Wilson from the National Council for the Traditional Arts organized The Cowboy Tour. A National Tour of cowboy songs, poetry, big windy stories, humor and fiddling. Nine cowboys representing different cattle-raising traditions traveled to cowtowns across the West, ranging from the Texas border to the Dakotas from the Montana badlands to the lush uplands of Hawai'i's Big Island. They recited cowboy poetry offering a glimpse into their lives and times, told jokes and big windy stories, sang in English, Spanish and Hawaiian and performed on fiddle, guitar, ukulele, and harmonica. Everett Brisendine, from Chino Valley, Arizona, was one of those nine cowboys on tour.

Strange as it may seem, cowboys appear to be the one of the few occupational groups in the United States with a high percentage of members who write and recite poetry. Glenn Ohrlin, another of the nine on the tour, recalled poetry as an interest of older cowboys who were on the Nevada range where he began buckarooing in 1943 at age 16. "Most of the old-timers didn't play guitar or even sing, but they knew songs. They'd recite songs just like they did poetry. Some had poems which were theirs. After awhile you knew them, but they were personal, so you'd never recite a man's poem without asking if you could."

In 1985 (January 31, Feb. 1-2) Hal Cannon, Jim Griffith and their crew held the first Cowboy Poets Gathering in Elko, Nevada. They invited 40 poets from 15 western states to recite poetry about ranch life in the West, to perform cowboy songs, and to discuss this genre of poetry. On September 2-4, 1988, the first Arizona Cowboy Poets Gathering was held at the Sheraton Resort and Conference Center (now the Prescott Resort) in Prescott, Arizona. The organizing committee members were Neil Abbott, Joe Austin, Sally Bates, Everett Brisendine, Don Charles, John Kennedy, Ross Knox, Warren Miller, Steve Rafters, Jeff Robertson, Joe Robertson, and Gail Steiger. 2004 marked the 20th anniversary of Elko, 2006 the 20th anniversary of the Texas Cowboy Poets Gathering, and 2007 marks the 20th anniversary of the Arizona Cowboy Poetry Gathering. No one envisioned that twenty years later we would still be doing the Gatherings. Cowboy poetry gatherings have become a cultural phenomenon attended by thousands of people every year and they've become a family reunion of sorts for the poets.

When these three gatherings started, one of the main goals was and still is to preserve cowboy poetry written by the classic poets such as Bruce Kiskaddon, Henry Herbert Knibbs, S. Omar Barker, Curly Fletcher, and Prescott's own Gail I. Gardner, and also that of contemporary working cowboy poets. (Kiskaddon, Fletcher, and Gardner all worked in and around Yavapai County.) Those who do the work and collect the pay as cowboys recognize what cowboy poetry is and that it is verse in rhyme and meter and tells the stories of, for, about and by cowboys and cowboy concerns and lifestyle. The content of these poems is something which you can't learn from a book or by watching Hollywood movies or television.

It probably isn't fair to ask why cowboys write cowboy poetry. A better question might be why did everybody else stop? Perhaps cowboys continue to write poetry because they have a deep respect for the habits and skills of old-timers in their profession; their verse is good and they enjoy it; they are people who are trained to keep an eye on what is going on around them and that is why cowboys make good poets; perhaps it is as simple as the fact that they are often alone and word fills up the quiet space. They write tales in rhyme and meter of the deeds and lifestyle, the family involvement, the ranch wife who survives without electricity, or the kids who have to entertain themselves. They put their heart on their sleeves and show you a side of the cowboy element you may never have heard before. They embrace family, friends, faith, and core values.

We thank all of our Arizona Cowboy Poets Gathering family—the volunteers, sponsors, committee members, Sharlot Hall Museum staff, host families, poets and spouses, and especially the public—who over the years have supported us. Without all of you, we would not be celebrating the 20th. As Audrey Hankins said, "The poem doesn't yield all of its riches on its first reading." We hope you have many happy "reads" because *Thanks for the Poems* is for all of you.

Mary and Nika

TABLE OF CONTENTS

THE MEN

* Empty Saddles

THE WOMEN
Arizona Poets

Neighboring Poets

Artwork By "Buckshot Dot"

*Empty Saddles

The idea for this book was birthed in 2005 and came to fruition in the minds and hearts of Mary Abbott, Sally Bates and Nika Nordbrock in March, 2006. Their hard work and efforts in behalf of the Prescott Gathering for many years are noteworthy, and this endeavor cements forever their hearts' desire to perpetuate the heritage of Cowboy Poetry. A heartfelt thanks to the rest of the selection committee: Neil Abbott, Dan Jarvis, Carole Jarvis, and Audrey Hankins.

Mary Abbott has been on the committee to produce the Prescott Gathering for the full 20 years. She and Neil have been the rudder that kept the gathering "on track" and "cowboy" as the years progressed and the audience changed. She's often found at gatherings around the West from Elko to Texas and loves the life she lives and her job as a working cowboy.

Nika Nordbrock has been the hardest working of all the committee members, no doubt. Very few are aware that this woman can put a whole passel of credentials behind her name! She holds a doctorate in linguistics and is an English instructor at Embry-Riddle Aeronautical University as well as having been employed at Sharlot Hall Museum.

Sally Bates is determined to perpetuate the culture and heritage of her family roots in the livestock industry, and the poetry that was part of her upbringing. That remains the driving force behind her involvement in the Gatherings.

The Men: Arizona Poets

SPELLBOUND

Lee Brimhall

When day is done on Burro Creek
I top out on the rim
And view the country far and wide
As day begins to dim.
Away off in the distance is
A mountain tall and steep
And I look out across that space
Of canyons wide and deep.

Away from town and city life
'Mid ruggcd rocks and hills
I hear the sound of night set in
And get a pleasant thrill.
Then back across the other way
A mountain looms up high
With granite peaks and ridges
That point up to the sky.

Side draws, slopes and turtlebacks
All shaped by nature's hand
To be there in the midst of it
The feeling sure is grand.
I realize how small I am
Comparcd to that vast land
And how to take good care of it
I try to understand.

I hear a night owl start to hoot
Then the call of a quail
A cow then bellows for her calf
Below her on the trail
While it's still light I look across
And view that canyon side
Where many times I've worked with stock
And where I soon will ride.

Continued . . .

To get down to the old ranch house
Before the night sets in
To rest up and be ready when
The new day will begin
My trusty steed has worked for me
All through the long hard day
And I dismount and sit a bit
As daylight fades away.

The sinking sun is almost gone
With western skies ablaze
And as I watch that setting sun
I sit there all amazed.
Those high and grassy mesas there
Above those canyons deep
Their picture in the setting sun
In memory I will keep.

I see a vast array out there
Of colors shades and hues
And I just sit there all entranced
Enjoying that awesome view.
That wild and rugged country there
Just stretches out for miles
And I think back how working there
Has had its hopes and trials.

The Great Creator sure must like
Wild country like that there
Because He made so much of it
With lots of it to spare.
Where stock will thrive if managed well
And wildlife do well too
For we improve the forage there
Because of what we do.

I hear a soft and rustling sound
Coming from the trees
And I feel things cool off a bit
Because of that mild breeze.
I know that my description just
Cannot tell the whole story
So I give thanks to artists who
Paint it in its full glory.

Then I mount up and head for home
But I am still spellbound
And soon I hear folks doing chores
And it's a welcome sound.
Then once again I think how much
I love that arid land
And how to live and work with it
Is where I make my stand!

STORE BOUGHT BUCKLE

Mike Dunn

He wears a store bought buckle . . .
  but he's cowboy through and through.
He rides, ropes, and wrangles,
  been thrown more than a time or two.

His younger years didn't allow the time
  to do the rodeo rounds.
On a working ranch, the oldest of five,
  he waited his turn to come around.

Too young, he became his dad's best hand,
  the responsibilities he accepted well.
For him, after school sports were fixing fence,
  feeding stock and milkin' the family cow.

He didn't play football or run the track,
  or play an instrument in the band,
His brothers and sisters did, while he
  took to ranching as he grew to be a man.

Riding, roping, and working stock,
  were things he had to know.
But when he displayed his skills,
  it wasn't for prizes or for show.

His efforts were out of necessity,
  helping to keep the ranch alive.
Each year, the next was to have been better
  and that would be his time.

He'd take off school for the gathering.
  he'd brand, mark, and cut.
He'd work as long and hard as any hand
  but never drew a check.

His dad gave him the old ranch truck
  to get around and do the chores.
It's then he started dating his sweethcart,
  when they were both sophomores.

He became an accomplished rancher
  by the time he'd finished school.
Managing, working and worrying,
  as a cowman's destined to do.

His brothers and sisters won the buckles,
  and his kids won more than their share.
When his time came it was for helping them
  and he was always there.

He rides, ropes, and wrangles,
  been thrown more than a time or two.
He wears a store bought buckle . . .
  but he's cowboy through and through.

FORGOTTEN WHEELS

Gail I. Gardner

From the cunning of the wheelwright
From the blacksmith's ringing stroke,
Built for use and built for service,
We were born of iron and oak.

Symphony of transportation
From the moving wagon train—
The strain and creak of leather,
And the jingling, swinging chain.

The hissing, cracking, popping
Of the slender black-snake whips,
The caustic, brimstone language
From the virile teamster's lips.

We have crossed the unbridged rivers,
We have rolled on prairie grass,
Slowly turning, we've ascended
To the snowy, lonely pass.

We've been rough-locked down the mountains,
Tires and felloe tightly chained;
We've been bogged hub-deep in 'dobe
While the steaming work-stock strained.

We're abandoned— we're forgotten,
In this field of final rest,
But our rolling, rolling, rolling,
Built the empire of the West.

LONG OF TOOTH

Dan Jarvis

When I was young and in my prime
I worked my buns off all the time.

Now that I'm older and I've got more sense,
I don't do windows, and I don't do fence.

I'm past the days of ridin' bogs
So I hang around the corral and train my dogs,

Or ride up in the hills and down the draw—
If I can't do it on a horse, I don't do it at all.

I don't flank calves or pitch no hay
Just sit on that horse, day after day.

I've got grass to find, and rivers to cross
There's no one around, so I pretend I'm boss.

I don't fix windmills, or prime no pumps,
I don't dig postholes, or pull out stumps.

I don't plow sod or put up hay,
I just straddle that old pony 'til the end of day.

I don't sleep on the ground with the snakes I dread,
I'm at home at night in my waterbed!

So if some of you punchers still in your prime,
Are scared of bein' caught by old father time,

I'm here to tell you that it's not all bad,
When you turn back the pages and see the fun you had.

And now that I've gotten "Long of Tooth"
And there's no callin' back the days of my youth,

I've got a Master's Degree in wrecks and spills,
So it's good to relax and just ride in the hills.

'Cause I've earned the title of a good buckaroo,
But there's some things left I still want to do.

But I ain't gonna' rush, I'll just take my time,
And do 'em all from the back of that old horse of mine!

9

DRY LIGHTNING

Bud Strom

*The year was 1994, the month of June, and we in Arizona could not pick up a
paper without seeing the drought-stricken Western States going up in uncon-
trolled wildfire. As I rode the west-most section and watched the clouds
gather, I thought about family, house and animals as the lightning struck the
hillsides; yet, no rain would follow. The threat of fire is with me each year
during our dry season.*

My day grows dim out makin' fence,
The buzzards circlin' high.
It's been like this the past six months,
The grass is tinder dry.

The cowmen sellin' off their herds,
The drought is very real.
This Arizona heat intense—
No rain—the land can't heal.

Ain't seen a drop fall from the sky
To land on pastures brown,
The cactus bent and shriveled up,
The mesquite hunkered down.

There's danger comes this time of year,
Late in the afternoon.
As thunderheads obscure the sky,
These days in late late June.

It's not the rain that threatens me,
It's that no rain will come,
As Zeus and Vulcan forge their bolts,
Apaches beat the drum.

Look up, expect the water spill,
From blackness all around.
To only see it disappear
Before it hits the ground.

It's that which pierces all of this,
That strikes my heart with fear.

Dry lightning in my mountain land,
Presents a danger clear.

Firewood cut from mountain slopes,
Brush piles beside the road;
A formula prescribed to work,
And ready to explode.

My cows are chummin' nervously,
Their calves are up and tight.
My horse a tremblin' stands his ground . . .
We watch the blindin' light.

A puff of smoke up canyon high,
My God, it strikes so near.
I know the devil winds will swirl,
And threaten all that's dear.

I close my eyes and pray this time,
That I am dreaming dreams.
No need for volunteers to show,
No need for sirens screams.

Well, this dry lightning passes now,
The slurry pilots rest:
Their planes can stay at idle . . .
No need to meet the test.

It will not spread beyond our means;
We give great thanks this day,
That "Hotshots" brave and fearless
Need not be in harm's way!

I sigh relief, my cows relax,
I spur my mount around.
Trees still thirst, grass stays hot,
But now we're homeward bound.

Tomorrow late, we'll be out there
Alert with all the strain
Of watching . . . waiting . . . silently
'Til dry lightning turns to rain.

ALL KINDS OF COWBOYS

Everett Brisendine

I could tell you a lot of stories
About Cowboys I have known
Some were dependable and steady
Others were always drifting, never knew a home

Some could tell the biggest windies
About the outfits they had run
How they rode them outlaw horses
And how fast they were with a gun

When you come into camp it started
On and on their stories ran
When that ol' cook uncovered them Dutchovens
They could really make a hand

Then you get into some rough country
Tryin' to turn a bunch of wild cows
You get your rope down and you're really spurrin'
But it looks like you ain't goin' to make it now

Then you think about them stories
They was a tellin' in camp last night
You keep lookin' back an' hopin'
But there ain't a dam' one in sight

But then I knew some others
That were solid as an Oak
They're always there to help you
Or to cheer you with a joke

They could tell you about horses
Could describe an ol' wild cow
Tell you what her calf looked like
And where she's runnin' now

They seemed to know about weather
Always lookin' at the moon
Could tell if it was wet or dry
And if Spring was comin' soon.

When you got in a game of poker
They always had what it took
Seemed to know when you were bluffin'
If you give your hole card a second look

They could use a long Riata
And they never missed a calf
And when everything was goin' wrong
They could always make you laugh.

Then I knew a couple others
With voices gruff and firm
Were about as bright and cheerful
As an ol' bull full of worms

From these ol' boys I learned a lot
And I rated them pretty high
An' when they talked you listened
'Cause they looked you in the eye

Lookin' back through memories
I think I've known some of the best
Some of these ol' boys were outstanding
They were the greatest in the West.

ZACK

Jim Dunham

He was one of my string when I hired out there,
One of five horses for my use and care.
At sixteen hands a big handsome black,
The horse wrangler said, "The boys called him Zack.
He's as good a cowhorse as I've ever seen,
Just the right teacher for someone that's green.
He knows this business, he'll outthink a cow,
What she's gonna do, just where, when, and how."

"He's easy to 'ketch, just call out his name,
You won't have to rope him, he's just that tame.
When you saddle him up, you'll sure get a ride,
There's plenty of horse beneath that old hide.
When you ride him, then ride him, and take a good seat.
Keep your mind in the middle and don't go to sleep,
'Cause he'll buck and he'll dump you, embarrass you, son,
He ain't mean nor vicious he's just havin fun."

We were workin' on Red Creek where the rocks are all pink,
I rode out in the water to let ol' Zack drink,
As he was a sippin' I was tryin to figger,
The ways of the women when he pulled the trigger.
He shied to the right, left me sittin' right there,
I lit flat on my face, came up gaspin' for air.
He was there on the creek bank, just as calm as could be,
And I swear that ol' jughead was grinnin' at me.

We were in the west pasture, on that malapais hill,
Pushin' a few head of cattle down toward the windmill.
When I spotted some mule deer, headin' out in a rush,
I leaned out in the saddle to look past some brush.
Zack bogged his ol' head and dumped me right there,
It tore up some hide and parted my hair.
When I looked for that cayuse he'd moved off just a tad,
And I think he was smilin', 'bout the fun he had had.

At a jackpot ropin' I once took a chance,
Thinkin' of greenbacks and the girls at the dance.
I built me a loop, just right for the task,
And nodded just once to ask for the calf.
That calf lit a runnin', he was haulin' the mail,
And ol' Zack was plum on him, right there on his tail.
But I'm still in the chute, layin' there on my back,
And the whole crowd is laughin', includin' Ol' Zack.

WAITIN' FOR SOME RAIN

Chris Isaacs

The coolness of the morning air
Hides well the bitter fact
That temperature means little
When the ground is dry and cracked.
Aspen leaves on Escudilla
Show their green against the sky,
But it's only nature's apparition
'Cause the stock tanks are all dry.

The older cows they know it's time
To move to summer range;
To green grass and easy livin',
They don't understand the change
That Mother Nature's dealt to us
These past six or seven years,
So we push them back to winter ground
And try to stifle fears.

Here it is the first of June
And we're still out here feedin' hay
And hopin' for a *red sky* every morning
As we start another day.
I saw cattle trucks pull into the Circle J,
Our nearest neighbor's place.
Guess they had all that they could take
Of this drought's dry embrace.

The radio said there's a chance for rain
In another week or two.
Guess we'll say a prayer, cross our fingers
And hope that that is true.
We'll bear down a little harder,
Do the work and bear the pain,
Watch for clouds, and haul more water
While we're waitin' for some rain.

16

VETS

Steve Lindsey

We was gathering cattle on the Concho,
      camped underneath the stars,
We'd followed the wagon out three days ago,
      A long way from pickups and cars.
"I can't believe I'm working on a wagon!"
      Heck, I was 19. . . just a kid!
Not many outfits used wagons now days
      but I's sure glad I worked for one that did!
I guess it was in my blood to be part of the chosen few.
My Daddy had worked on a wagon,
      and my Grandpa and great Grandpa too.

I was sure enjoying my freedom! The good ole US of A!
I didn't have a care in the world
      and I figured it'd stay that way.
I had just crawled into my bedroll,
      I was snuggling down there real deep,
Thinking about the next day's gatherin'
      just about off in my sleep,
When I sure thought that I seen something,
      but like Saint Peter I's off in a trance;
Then I saw someone standing there
      in a green Army uniform,
      and somehow I knew he was somewhere in France.

And I knew that it was my Grandpa,
      though I'd never met him before,
He was one of the first ones to land on D-Day,
      and he'd died on that Normandy shore.
He seemed to look right through me,
      like he knew who I was too,
Then he started talking to me just like I'm talking to you.

Continued . . .

17

He said, "Son I know you're enjoying your freedom,
        cuz I've been were you are tonight,
Working on a wagon in the American West
        looking at a billion stars givin' their light.
But for you to be enjoying your freedom,
        some had to fight and some died,
And thousands more was willing to go,
         and hundreds of wives
          and golden star mothers have cried.

Your Great Grandpa fought in the trenches in WWI,
         and I died under this Normandy dam,
Your Uncle fought in Korea,
        and your Daddy in Vietnam.
Even ole' Cookie fought in Vietnam,
        you've heard him talk of his beloved Marine Corps
But he got shot up when he was over there
        and he can't set a horse no more.
And them kids you went to school with
        that joined the military,
        they're fightin' somewhere in Iraq,
Tryin' to extend the American dream,
        and we don't know when they're coming back!

All for the right of your freedom
        so you'd have the right to choose,
So's you could stand up and say what you want,
        and boy that's something you don't wanna lose!
So while you're enjoying your freedom,
        you need to thank a Vet.
They're the ones that bought it for you
        with tears and blood and sweat!"

Then just like he came he was gone,
        my Grandpa went back to his grave,
But I'll never forget that night's visit,
        and all of the wisdom he gave.

And God Bless all of you American veterans!
I take my hat off to you!
Thanks for all that you've done,
and all that you were willing to do!

Oh say does that Star Spangled Banner yet wave
Over the land of the free, and the home of the brave.

WEANIN' TIME

Neil Abbott

It's weanin' time
It's awful noisy now
Every place you listen
You hear the bawlin' of a cow.

Now those calves that we weaned
Were all big and stout
But these cows here a bellerin'
Don't know that they can do without.

The trucks are gone now
The calves are on the way
And the cows ain't payin' no attention
To the water or the hay.

The nearest fences
Are sure to be wiped out
But those cows still don't know
Them calves can do without.

It's been a long, dry summer
It was bad you can bet on that
But always that cow knew
Just where that calf was at.

I 'member that old brockie
She hid her calf real well
And when I went checkin' cattle
She gave the dogs pure hell.

And the Brahmie
She calved a way up high
That calf he thought he was
A'kin to the buzzards in the sky.

And that Hereford
Her calf came the wrong way
If I hadn't come along
Maybe they wouldn't have made it, who's to say?

It'll be quiet soon
At least by the third day
And then it'll just be me
The dogs and old grey.

WHERE DO WE GO FROM HERE

Phil Ellsworth

I left this mornin' early on. I don't much like good byes.
The Boss was up and shook my hand,
I saw friendship in his eyes.

He said he's sorry to see me go, but I said I might be back
He said he knew just how I felt,
He'd traveled a similar track.

Now, lookin' back, it warn't so bad.
In fact, it was pretty good.
I enjoyed the time spent there, and did everything I could.

The country there was kind, with water, grass and land,
I can't think of a better place
For a Cowboy to give a hand.

It sure 'nuf was cow country, the cattle fat and sleek.
All a man could ask for.
So now what do I seek?

I tell you there's an itch, that this Cowboy has to scratch.
I can stay a place for just so long, before I have to pack.

I guess I always yearn, to see the other side,
Of hills and mountains tall, across the great divide.

I take my buddies, Jim, Jake and Bo.
There's places we've gotta' see.
Whether it's hills, or plains or cactus,
Or the range beside the sea.

I suppose I'll settle down someday. Maybe someplace near.
For now though, the question is,
"Where do we go from here?"

THE RODEO RIDER AND THE BUCKAROO

Robert Reynvann

 I was sittin' at the Palace Bar one July afternoon,
I was listenin' to this rodeo rider,
he was makin' all the girls swoon.
His hat was clean and styled nice,
his shirt was white as snow.
He wore a buckle the size of a dinner plate,
and his boots had a blindin' glow.
He was braggin' about the buckin' hosses
and rodeos he had rode,
And saying the life of a buckaroo
is the only life he knows.
He was sayin' how tough the circuit was
and how he could get hurt.
I just set there listenin' and lookin' at his spotless shirt.

Well, I guess he heard me chucklin',
and it must have made him mad,
'Cause he walked up to me and said,
"Old man . . . I'm BAD."
I smiled and said, "I meant no harm,
I'm just listenin' to your bull.
There's no doubt you're a rodeo rider,
but you've got no buckaroo pull.
You crawl down on a buckin' horse
with the buck rein in your hand,
Your hat pulled down, your cinch is tight,
and you know you're a rodeo man.
You got the word from all you friends
just how that horse will buck,
And your hopin' you'll be in the money soon
with just a little luck.

Continued . . .

With a doctor and an ambulance standin' by,
and the arena plowed just right,
The only thought on your mind
is to spur with all your might.
You nod your head, they open the gate,
and the horse comes out with a dash,
He tucks his head and kicks his feet,
and eight seconds go by in a flash.
The whistle blows, a man rides up
on a fancy painted horse,
He grabs the flank cinch, you grab his waist,
the ride is over, of course.
The crowd cheers as you tip your hat
and walk back to the chute.
Plumb proud of yourself for a high score ride,
and you didn't even scuff a boot.

Well, a Buckaroo's life is not that way,
for life's a little different you know.
There ain't no doctors, or pickup man,
when you horse decides to blow.
You're usually in a granite rock pile,
twenty-five miles from camp.
Standin' in the stirrups
with a catch rope in your hand.
You got thirty feet of clearin'
betwixt the cholla and the prickly pears,
And that's when this half-broke saddle hoss
decides to throw you there.
His head goes down and you drop your rope,
and your heart pumps an extra spurt,
You know from the past if he beds you down here
you're damn sure gonna be hurt.

You grab for leather and pull one rein,
try to get his head around,
And all this time you're doin' your best
to keep your butt off the ground.
Well, it ain't real pretty and it ain't real smooth
but no one's keepin' score
You're doin' your best to stay aboard
'cause there ain't no crowds to roar.
There ain't nobody watchin' at all,
there's just you and that bronc of course
And, the nastiest four words that a buckaroo knows is,
"Somebody catch my horse!"
Now I ain't takin' nothing from 'ya,
cause you are a Rodeo Cowboy through and true.
But before you call yourself a Buckaroo,
I suggest you pay up a few dues.

THE "EYES" HAVE IT

Rolf Flake

Well, I went to see the Banker
To borrow me some "dough,"
I went with fear and trembling
Afraid he'd tell me "No."

But the Banker, he surprised me
Said, "I'll tell you what I'll do,
I have one glass eye, if you can tell which
I'll just make that loan to you."

I'm sure that he done this before
With many an unsuspecting "catch,"
And I'm sure he'd won more times than lost
'Cause his eyes were so well-matched.

Which eye was glass? How could I tell?
But then I saw the light!
"It's that one sir, I'm sure it is,
The one that's on your right."

Well, the Banker he was startled
That I could tell so fast.
Said, "I'll keep my word, you got the loan,
But tell me, how did you guess?"

"Well, sir," I said, "'twas easy,
I figured it in this fashion,
The one on the right, the glass one,
Has just a glimmer of compassion."

A GOOD RIDE

Dean Cook

It's happened to us all; it'll never fail,
I was dozing in the saddle on that desert trail
When that old Shorty horse saw his chance,
And dropped his head and asked me to dance.

He almost lost me the very first jump
There was inches of daylight 'tween saddle and rump
I lost a stirrup, and I lost a rein
So I grabbed some leather and I grabbed some mane.

It was not a thing of beauty or grace
And I was hoping nobody had seen my disgrace
When the trail boss yelled from the other side,
"If you stay on top, it's a good ride!"

If you stay on top, it's a good ride
It's about survival, and not just pride
So grab some leather or grab some hide
If you stay on top, then it's a good ride!

He said, "Here's one thing that I know,
You can't confuse life with rodeo.
'Cuz 8 seconds won't get you in our record book,
And we don't give points for how you look."

So when some hell breaks loose and you're headed for a wreck,
You may have to choose between your pride and your neck.
Then you can pull leather and lose some face
Or you can get thrown with style and grace.
But here's a thing that I have found,
Nobody looks good when they hit the ground.

If you stay on top, it's a good ride
It's about survival, and not just pride
So grab some leather and grab some hide,
If you stay on top, it's a good ride!

THE SMELL OF WOOD SMOKE

Tommy Thomas

Do you recall toppin' the canyon rim
    on a crystal clear winter night?
The full moon ridin' high, fresh snow layin' soft and white.
The lamp in the bunkhouse window in the valley far below
Casts its soft yellow welcome on the freshly fallen snow.

The smoke curls from the bunkhouse chimney
But you still got a long way to go.
Then you catch a whiff of the wood smoke
Through the pine trees white with snow.

It stirs your blood and your memories
As you spur your hoss to a trot.
You smell the fragrance of the wood smoke.
You can't wait for that ol' coffeepot.

You recall spring round up at the wagon
When ol' cookie was fixin' some chuck.
The smoke an' the sparks was a-flyin'
And your ol' pony broke into a buck.

Then there's those spring nights after branding
Burning hair and dust sting your nose.
You look at the stars from your bedroll;
The smell of wood smoke drifts from your clothes.

And the time we was camped on the desert
Where we ran out of wood for fuel,
An ol' cookie started usin' some cowchips
Man—that would give asthma to a mule.

Then the times you were lookin' for cattle
On the mountain—in the pines tall and thick
When a fierce lightnin' storm had just started a fire
Then the smell of pine smoke sorta' makes you sick.

But most times the smell of the wood smoke
Made you happy and really glad,
As it brought back so many memories
Of the best times you've ever had.

Like the great times after supper
And the boys would be spinnin' yarns 'round the fire
I've wondered if sniffin' too much wood smoke
Could make an honest hand a real number one liar!

To a cowboy there ain't no store bought perfume
That he likes or smells half as sweet
As when he's hungry as a half-starved grizzly bear
An ol' cookie is cookin' with mesquite.

I was also thinkin' back to my boyhood days
When I was just a young cowpoke.
The fragrance of my mom's kitchen, and
The smell of fresh bread, pies and wood smoke.

Well—most of these things are gone now
And young folks may think it's a joke,
When some of us older punchers get sentimental
About simple things like the smell of wood smoke.

And ain't it kinda' funny
How in memory you can recall
Things that to most seem unimportant
And to many they're worthless and small.

Now, if you see an ol' cowboy 'round the campfire
With a far away look in his eyes
Don't bother to ask what he's athinkin'
He's not dreamin' up big windies or lies.

He could probably go on for hours
With his memories from out of the past
All the hosses an' men that he's known
And how time flies so very fast.

He recalls the hoss tracks he's left on this land
And though now he may be rich or broke
All these long trails he's re-living now
As he gazes at the fire, and smells the wood smoke.

THANKS FOR THE POEM

Tom Weathers

He'd been rastl'n a mood, that set him a brood'n
Trying to figure what this life's trail's about
But instead of just frettin', to a poem he starts settin'
Some rhymes to help sort it all out.

At the head of the sheet is the name and the street
Where he bathes and beds down when in town
And though the pages were white, when he started to write,
They're now become, more finger smudged brown.

For the lines, they come slow, and the cowboy don't know
When the next inspiration might hit
So he carefully pens, even the least unction when
A piece to this wrote puzzle might fit.

It's a tally he's takin' as each new day's breakin'
That he fashions to rhyme in his head
Then in dusk's fading light he commences to write
His trails account, which 'til now'd gone unsaid.

There's some thoughts that fly by, with but a heartbeat to try
To lass' it and dally up with a pen
Into a simply put line, set to meter and rhyme
How he feels when a new day begins.

And some thought plod along, not much flash, but so strong
'Bout the ties his life holds with the soil
And the hills, and the rain, the grass covered plain
Making pleasure from what others call toil

Now his daily subjection, to this written reflection
In anecdotes current and past
Had in time reached such number
    that one night, fighting slumber
He set to reading them all, first to last.

And as the verses unwound, him setting there on the ground
He took to seeing his life, like his rhymes
For if that tales to be told it needs be taken in its whole
To make sense, not just verse at a time.

'Cause though life's lived bit by bit to make sense out of it
The trail needs be judged by its whole
There'll be drought, there'll be rain,
    maybe glory and some shame
But the end of life's trail its goal.

Well that thought brought a grin,
    'cause now the blowdown he's in
Didn't seem where he'd always need roam
Then, with a glint in his eye he tipped his hat to the sky
And told his maker, *"Thanks for the poem."*

THE BARN ON THE BAR D

Shag Reimer

I stopped to rest my horse one hot summer day,
We stood in the shade, my thoughts on instant replay.
I traveled down that dirt road on the edge of town,
And a smile on my face replaced the frown.

Things are taking shape, this is no spoof,
I see the peeling whitewash and the rusty tin roof.
Back across the yard is that old horse barn,
Without it this wouldn't be much of a yarn.

It had two rows of stalls, one down each side,
Each filled with a horse that brought much pride.
The sides were kind of long and low,
With a high breezeway for hay to stow.

The dusty old rafters and last year's hay,
And a smell of horses that won't go away.
It had a back gate that was always out of plumb,
Just to close it was a challenge for some.

With fly-specked lights always a welcome sight
That watched the birth of colts that came in the night,
Even a calendar girl with a smiling face,
And a single spur I had stuck in a brace.

Some old horseshoes tacked up on the wall,
Each one a story, some short, some tall.
This was home for things with hair and feather,
A tack room full of saddles, the smell of sweaty leather.

Late one night we were all asleep in bed,
Someone shouted "Fire!" loud enough to wake the dead
I looked out the window, still in a daze,
The whole dam' barn looked to be ablaze!

A shout was heard, "Let's get the horses out!"
While others sprayed water from a leaky old spout.
In I went with a wet sack over my head,
Hoping to God the horses weren't dead.

We covered their eyes with wet feed sacks,
Led them out the doors, did we make tracks!
Out they came, one at a time,
Tied them on the fence in a long line.

The stall doors stood open, the horses were out,
It was time to give thanks and shout.
Then old Dutchess pulled back and broke her rope,
She headed back in all that fire and smoke.

Just as she went into the flames, smoke and all,
That red hot tin roof started to fall.
Then it caved in with a mighty roar,
All the roof and hay crashed to the floor.

By the back fence we sat in our places,
In silence we watched with tears on our faces.
Now the blaze had pretty much died down,
And the old fire truck headed back to town.

The sun was up and it was a new day,
We headed for the house with nothing to say.
Then we heard my Uncle say, "Well, kiss my ass!"
Out on the lawn was Dutchess, calmly eating grass!

*All we could figure is that she ran out the other side as the roof began
to fall. She was one of my Uncle's best broodmares, so he was sure
thankful.*

WISHIN'

A young cowboy stands, with his hat pulled down low
Straddle his stick horse, sure wishin' he could go
On the gather with dad, down by the springs
But he's still just too young to do these kind of things.

In his mind he could ride from daylight til' dark
Heck, in his dreams, why that weren't even a start!
Why, he'd gathered cattle out of brush
    so thick you couldn't see
Just like his dad, a hand someday he'd be.

And just like his grandpa, the broncs he would ride
He'd swing a wide loop, ain't nothing' he wouldn't try.
His legs are too short and his legging's too long
They drag 'bout six inches behind, as he gallops along.

Across the yard he rides at a break-neck speed
Trustin' life and limb, to his rarest of steeds
There's not even a chance for the outlaws these days
They'd better be huntin' new country
    or changing' their ways!

'Cause this hombre is tough, or soon someday will be
As I turn in the saddle, lookin' back I can see
That little young cowboy reminds me . . . Of me.

"Like This Grandpa?" by Norm Deitchman

RIDIN' FOR THE BRAND

Weldon Rutledge

There's a sayin' in cattle country,
It's called "ridin' for the brand,"
It's known by all cowpunchers,
Who are any kind of hand.

"Ridin' for the brand" means loyalty,
To the outfit where you work,
It means true dedication,
To a job you never shirk.

It means when things get stormy,
And it's tough to make a hand,
It means you bare your teeth and "cowboy up,"
So you can "ride for the brand."

It means that when an old wild cow,
Leaves the holdup in a rush,
It means you go and catch her,
Before she gets into the brush.

It means you lead her back,
On the end of your rope,
It means if you can't do it, for you,
There's not much hope.

When the outlaws tried to "cut the herd,"
It meant you might have to fight,
It meant you stand up by the trail boss,
Without showin' any fright.

It meant you pull your "hogleg,"
And join in the fight,
It meant nobody cuts the herd,
That we're guardin' day and night.

Continued . . .

I've ridden for the Pothook's,
And the brand called Slash I Bar,
I've ridden for the Four P's,
And a lot of others near and far.

But the brand we need to ride for,
'Cause they're in an awful mess,
The terrorists are tryin' to cut the herd,
Of the brand we call U.S.

This fight don't need to last no longer,
It's already taken its toll,
We all need to pull our "hoglegs,"
"Cowboy up" and say "Let's roll."

Some don't even know the meanin',
Of "ridin' for the brand."
Some never heard of loyalty,
Like we know in Cowboy land.

I feel sorry for all the people,
Who never knew about the code,
That us hired men on horseback have,
And 'bout all the horses that we've rode.

It has a lotta different meanings,
Out here in the western land,
But no matter how you phrase it,
It still means "ridin' for the brand."

This poem is dedicated to President George W. Bush,
the rescue workers at WTC, N.Y.P.D., N.Y.F.D. and all
of the men and women serving in the Armed Forces,
who are all "Ridin' for the Brand" - the US Brand!

AFTERNOON RAIN

Bill Beam

Standin' outside the 'dobe
Lookin' south across the line,
Lightnin' flashed through the heavens,
'Twas the first warnin' sign.

'Round the top of San Jose
Black clouds began to roll.
I hear the distant rumble
Of the storms heart and soul.

Cottonwood leaves now flutter
As dust begins to blow,
Ol' windmill starts to spinnin'
Pumpin' water from below.

Horses begin to spook
In the cross tie corral,
As the wind 'n' dust roar
Like the open gates o' Hell.

Suddenly the downpour comes
With fury an' deafinin' roar,
Ya' swear to God ya' never
Saw it rain like this before.

Just as quickly as she came
The storm has gone on by
Air smells fresh an' clean
'Neath the Arizona sky.

Arroyos run from bank to bank
With mud 'n' froth an' such
Then suddenly they're empty
As if by magic touch.

Continued . . .

Ol' sun is burnin' brightly
Desert's quiet once again,
And I can hardly wait
For the next afternoon rain!

DREAM OF THE PRAIRIE

Buck Ryberg

Dream of the prairie— dream of the wildwind
Dream of the grasses belly high
Dream of the old days— dream of the riders
They lope beneath the endless prairie sky.

My cowboy days are over,
My glory days are gone
No more dusty days upon the trail
Beneath a hazy sun.
All that I can do is dream my dreams
And in my mind there's one more ride
A good strong horse between my legs
We roam the prairie stride by stride.

Last night I laid my bedroll down
One more time beneath the moon
There I took my old guitar
And I played a prairie tune
I heard the riders comin' hard
I heard their mournful cry
You might say it was the prairie wind
But I saw 'em ridin' by.

Bury me upon the lone prairie
Where tumbleweeds are tumblin' down
I hope blue shadows steal across the trail
And cool water's all around
Sing a song about old San Antone
Dance a step with glistened eye
Then turn away and leave me all alone
Out on the prairie I will fly

Then sing of the prairie— sing of the wildwind
Sing of the grasses belly high
And sing of the old days— sing of the riders
They lope beneath the endless prairie sky.

MONARCH OF THE RANGE

Carson Thomas

Standin' out in the wagon yard,
Old . . . Weathered . . . and darn sure saggin'
Is the form of what once was
A mighty fine chuck wagon

It shows the years of workin' hard
And if that old rig could talk
What a story it would tell boys
Why, it would probably stop a clock

That old spring seat is broken down
And leans mighty far to the right
That old wagon box is cracked and dried underneath
Where many a hand spent the night

Well, them old wood bows still hold their shape
And have stood the test of time
But the tarp for many years is gone
From the weather it's not been kind

The brake handle is worn from the sole of a boot
From the many miles that it has traveled
The fly tarp ropes have all but rotted
And the rest have just come unraveled.

The jockey box hangs from the front of the wagon
And still holds some old wagon tools
The tongue is straight, and it's fair to say
It's been pulled by horses and some mules.

The water barrel bands have slipped out of place
Where once they were good and tight
The paint is all but faded away
When it was new, it was green, red, real bright

At the back of the wagon where the chuckbox hangs
A many good meal was built
Like biscuits, beef and beans
And coffee that would give you a jilt

Them old wheels have turned a million miles
Following cattle tracks across this land
This wagon has run on some top outfits
As its box carries many a good brand

As the years take its toll on the old runnin' gear
And the double trees hang there in space
Chances are it's rolled its last round up
This could be its final restin' place

It's been through the rain
The snow and the drought
It's run on the North range
It's run on the South

It's been home to the cowboy
And the buckaroo
And even to a few
Ole cranky cooks or two

It's the headquarters for the roundup
Throughout the spring and fall
And those cowboys would come a ridin'
When that old cookie'd call

Like a castle to a king it was
For all the boys alike
Home was wherever it was
Didn't matter day or night

But when the work is over
And the wagon is in the yard
I get this strange sick feelin'
You've had it too, haven't you, pard?

Continued . . .

That next year when that wagon rolls
It sure could be its last
As we're livin' in an age
That is just dyin' way too fast

So I just pray for one more year
To see a wagon track
And when I do, I'll say, "Thank you."
And darn sure tip my hat.

FLIES

Chuck Lakin

Friends, have you ever wondered why
The years so swiftly hurry by?
Of times long gone, we often say,
"It seems like only yesterday."

Now, you may find this hard to buy,
But it's caused by a certain kind of fly.
An entomologist I'll never be
But I'm an expert on "fly-ology."

And since we'll never be without 'em
I'll tell you a little bit about 'em:
It's in the good book, you'll find his name,
A dude named Noah is the guy to blame.

When Noah loaded the Ark that day,
He must've been lookin' the other way
Surely he didn't realize
He'd let in all those pesky flies!

They're nasty things, and a nuisance too,
And they cost us billions in revenue.
Think of the trouble he could avert
Had he been a little bit more alert!

House flies speck the window pane
And drive the horses near insane.
Face flies make the cows lose weight
And cause their tails to flagellate.

Screw worm flies, the rancher's hex
Met their demise from sterile sex.
The heel fly damages the hide,
Which the tannery cannot abide.

Continued . . .

43

he bot fly puts your horse to flight,
And causes internal parasites.
The nit fly covers his legs with nits,
And sometimes makes him throw a fit.

The horsefly makes him buck and pitch
When you try to swat the sumabich!
The blow fly blows that stinky carrion,
Stuff that's bad in need of buryin'.

White flies are tiny, cute and sexy
But they give the farmers apoplexy,
And there's a thousand, million, zillion of 'em.
Which makes it awful hard to love 'em.

But now, friends, I want your full attention
The worst kind of flies I've yet to mention.
TIME FLIES, is their common name,
And eating calendars is their game.

They eat the months and they eat the years
And they make the decades disappear,
And friends it's because of them we so often say,
"It seems like only yesterday."

SCHOOLMARMS AND COWBOYS

Larry Harmer

There's something sort of odd
I've noticed her of late
Seems like a lot of cowboys have
Taken a schoolmarm as their mate.

Now, some folks think the cowboy
As not altogether too bright,
But he was bright enough to marry
A smart woman as his wife.

Maybe it was his schoolboy charm
Or the shufflin' of his feet,
As he lowers his eyes and tips his hat
In an act of shy defeat.

But, whatever may have been his method,
Or whatever may have been his way
He managed to come out on top
In looks . . . and brains . . . and probably even pay!

But I can't help sort'a thinkin'
If because all others he must forsake,
He may as well get a smart one . . .
It's the last decision he gets to make!

MEMORIES

Ross Knox

You sit in your chair and you stare at the wall
You re-live the days when you rode proud and tall
While making the big drives; rope and brand
And just practice the art of making a hand.

You was just a kid when you left your home
And headed north to the Yellowstone
To those high mountain meadows in a pristine land
That's yet to be ruined by human hand.

It still brings a smile when you re-live the ride
On a moonlit night across the great divide
With the Northern Lights sparkling like diamonds and jewels
Just you, and God and a string of mules.

You made your camp up on Two Ocean creek
You let the sound of the water sing you to sleep.
And those high desert ranches on the Nevada range
Where for the last hundred years there's been dam' little
    change.

At night, round the chuck wagon you wish folks could see
That you and the mustang the only thing left that's free
From a hilltop you'd stare at the vast expanses
Seemed you could trot forever and hit no fences.

With no time clock or desk each day we'd thank God
That we're not a slave to the urban mob.
Yes, you'd chosen to ride a trail seldom traveled
Little knowing how fast it can all come unraveled.

Remember the winter of '73,
The beginning of the end for men like me.
You were on top of the world and then overnight
The cow market dropped clear out of sight.

It just kept getting' worse with each passing day
Till a cow wasn't hardly worth giving away.
You'd spent your whole life keeping a tradition alive
Now each day is a constant battle to just try and survive.

But, though the cost of grass keeps going up
And cow prices keep falling
Being a cowboy is still the highest calling

Now, you're a prisoner to a chair that has wheels
But you still remember the way that it feels
To step across a good horse and a custom made saddle
The thrill of running mustangs or tying down wild cattle

For the last forty years you've had the same loving wife
There's not much you'd change about your life
But, when the memories come calling,
    you still can't help but pray,
Lord, please make me a cowboy again for a day.

For Buck, for Sunny, for Larry, for J.B. For the rest of the crew that has been called home. I guess God needed you more than we did. We'll see you soon.

THE YOUNG HORSE

Frank Rodriques

The young horse stands in the hobbles,
As he soaks beneath the saddle.
The cowboy straps on his leggings,
As he prepares for the battle.

He steps to the stirrup,
As he reins the horse up tight.
Then he molds his body in the saddle,
And prepares for the fight.

A few seconds pass,
Like a stoplight on the street
Then the young horse went to buckin'
Trying to throw the rider from his seat.

Buckin' in a circle,
With his head pulled 'round
Then started crow hoppin'
Trying to put the rider down.

The cowboy slapped him on the rump,
Then spurred him in the shoulder
But the young horse kept on buckin'
And gettin' even bolder.

With all fours
He went straight up in the air
Creating quite a dust bowl
On the ground below him there.

He put his nose between his front legs
As his hind legs scratched the sky
Trying to get rid of his rider,
Like a bird— watch him fly.

Continued . . .

But his rider had control
And stayed there in the seat
As the young horse kept buckin'
Showing the sun the soles of his feet.

With a white, foamy body
He gave to the bit
Then surrendered to the cowboy
From having a wall-eyed fit.

Now he's walking peaceful,
And listens to commands
As the cowboy reins him gentle
And pets him with his hands.

Now the days have come and gone
And I'm sure that you'll agree
He still gets a little burr
Whenever there's a cold and frosty breeze.

The Women: Arizona Poets

Artwork by Lynn Brown

A LEAP OF FAITH

Sally Bates

When your left foot hits the stirrup
And your right foot leaves the ground
There's a whole lot that can happen
While your butt is saddle bound!

It's a leap of faith you're takin'
As you reach toward the crest
That this horse you're takin' holt of
Will respond with all his best.

There's a vast pool of potential
In that space between his ears
And a cowboy knows he's reachin'
For what lies beyond the fears.

So you watch his eyes for tension
As you catch hold of the mane
Then your left foot hits the stirrup
While you try to read his brain.

And you see yourself reflected
In the window of his soul
But your toe has found position
In foundation with a hole.

And what happens in that moment
When your right foot leaves the ground
Will either make or break you
If his choice is come unwound.

But you've surely done your groundwork
And this isn't his first round
Where a left foot hit the stirrup
And a right foot left the ground.

So you take that leap of faith again
Where hope and hard work meet
With a sense that all the world is right
In the rhythm of his feet.

53

CACTUS, SAND AND STONE

Shawn Cameron

There's a wretched, wicked region
Of the cactus, sand and stone,
Where time's an endless season . . .
And man's spirit's free to roam.

Here, the soul is but a whisper
Floating swift across the land
Sharing secrets with Saguaros
Who stand sentinel and grand.

It celebrates the barrels
Who bloom through discontent . . .
For they are born survivors
And stay true to their intent.

In this hot and prickly region
Of the cactus, sand and stone
The eastern sky is warming
As a horseman rides alone.

In the coolness of the hour
He sets hoof upon the ground . . .
Striding long across a landscape
As far melodies resound.

The morning dove is cooin'
And the Gambel's Quail now call
To the coyote who is wailing . . .
At the magic of it all.

The horseman, now, is leaning
As he trots along the trail
Watching close, and waiting . . .
For the signs that will not fail.

The branches that are broken . . .
And the imprints in the sand
Will tell the tale of cattle
Who, here, have taken stand.

Soon . . . all's quiet in the desert
And the songs of sunrise cease
No sound is heard descending
As the canyon walls increase.

Now, a splash of color casting
In the shadows dark and dim
Below the beaned mesquite trees
Underneath the canyon's rim.

There, sheltered from sensations
Of a sultry, smoldering sky
Stand the horned and painted legends
Of historic tales gone by.

They're survivors of the desert
A mere mystery of the land,
Whose beauty's as deceptive
As the sparkling, sunlit sand.

There's a toughness to the spirit
And yet a sinewed grace
In these cattle of the cowboy
That indwell this desert place.

The cowboy's found his purpose,
Where the granite spires are sheer
And the water trickles downward
Toward grasses growing near.

In this wanting, writhing region
Of the crucifixion thorn
There are souls that share a secret . . .
Here a kindred spirit's born.

Corrientes and the cowboy
Rooted deep in mystery lore
Share the secret of the desert
To survive . . . a season more.

STILL DOIN' BUSINESS

Bunny Dryden

Coffee sputters from the camp pot
Aroma wafts upon the morn
4 am . . . it's time for rising
As another day is born.

One more chance to live the good life
Sit the saddle, ride the range
For upon each dawn is riding
Subtle hints of coming change.

One hundred years stands in-between us;
Family ranchers and those who don't.
We're a dying breed there's no doubt
Giving up, we surely won't.

Weathered faces, calloused rough hands
Battle wounds were earned with pride
Scrapes and scratches; rope burns; blisters,
It's for the HD brand we ride.

Numbers cut, just breaking even
Can't make a living off the herd
So to keep our family heritage,
"Diversification" is the word.

Cattle ranching has some new stock,
Two-legged breed instead of four
Guess what we got is pretty special,
'Cause they keep coming back for more.

Breathe the clean air; see the sunset;
Watch a Black Hawk as it soars,
Quiet thought with peaceful pleasure,
Away from constant city roars.

We've hung on through waves of hatred
For running cattle on the land
Kept the wild and open spaces
Untouched by developmental hands.

Be a cowboy just for one day
Live the dream of yesteryear
Even if it's not forever
You can be a cowboy here.

Light the fire; sort the cattle;
Bellering-bawls singeing the air.
Stamp the brand and cut the earmark,
Burning eyes from smoking hair.

Make a round to check for stragglers
Busting brush through rugged trails
Something stirs out in the distance,
Stubborn family pride prevails.

Mother cow and calf beside her
In the brush upon the hill
Drive 'em in through catclaw, cactus;
Yeah— we're doing business still.

A ROAST AND A POT OF BEANS

Audrey Hankins

In the kitchen on most any ranch
There's always good food it seems,
But my all-time overall favorite
Is a roast and a pot of beans.

You can put them on in crockpots
The handy, liberated way,
Then go off to town on business
Or to the backside and ride all day.

That moist, mouthwatering aroma
Drifts right down the road it seems
And draws you home to the kitchen
That roast and a pot of beans.

Set out bread, butter and salsa,
And chocolate cake for dessert,
Then watch those cowboy eat
'Til you know they've got to hurt.

This morning we're shipping
And short-handed it seems.
So saddle my horse, while I put on
A roast and a pot of beans.

RAIN

Janet Moore

I watch it glide over the mountains,
Life giving moisture is rare
In this desert country,
There's never enough anywhere.

I breath a prayer for its blessing
As I watch it touch the ground
Thirsty and waiting to blossom
Enjoying its smell and its sound.

In the evening after the storm passed
I watched the sun's setting rays
Turn clouds into celebration
In various pink and crimson shades.

I'll sleep better tonight for just knowing
Moisture has touched the earth
And God has blessed us one more time
With the grasses and floral rebirths.

OUR DESTINY

Daisy Dillard

We were both very young when we married
I was barely seventeen
We had no idea what life was about,
But our heads and hearts were filled with dreams.

We worked from one ranch to another
Sometimes life got pretty tough
But our heads and hearts wanted to ranch
Seemed we just couldn't get enough.

No matter how low the wages
No matter how hard the times might be
Ranchin' was in our very souls
It was to be our destiny.

We tried livin' in town doin' other jobs
But somehow they never seemed to work out
Ranchin' was always callin' to us
Till the call would become a shout.

For many years we worked other men's spreads
And took care of them like they were our own
No matter how good or run down things were
We managed to make the place home.

Sometimes I hated patchin' britches
And washin' clothes on the ol' rub board.
Meals didn't come in boxes
And a Super Market wasn't right out the door.

We were young, and we were foolish
In some of the decisions that we made
Left some places for what seemed greener pastures
When we'd been better off to have stayed.

But I wouldn't trade one minute
Of the lifetime that we've spent
For all of the riches on this earth
In the monetary sense.

For each patch that I was a sewin'
Was put on with love and care
And the mem'ries that come back to me now
I wouldn't trade with a millionaire.

RANCH WIDOW

Marge Tucker-Woodhurst

You have heard of the ranch widow
A poor, long suffering colleen
She has a husband who lives on the ranch
And is seldom ever seen.

While she has a house in town
To put the kids in school
Getting together on weekends
Is usually the general rule.

Then there's the other ranch widow
Who stays home on the place
While her husband works on a far-off ranch
And she seldom sees his face.

He has to work away from home
To feed his cows and children
Taking care of another man's cows
'Cuz that's the only thing he's skilled in.

He has to pay the mortgage
Buy materials for new fence
He's building for the future,
And that makes a lot of sense.

So the ranch widow stays at home,
'Cuz she really is stuck
Unless she wants to walk to town,
Her husband has the truck!

She cleans the barn and feeds the calves
After she's milked the cow
And throws hay down to the horses
From the old hay mow.

She splits some wood for the cook stove
And for the fireplace too,
Gathers eggs and churns butter
And she is almost through.

When she hears the clatter of a truck,
Sounds very like her own
Yep, here it comes down off the hill
Her husband has come home.

He needs a shave and haircut
But he still looks mighty good
"I had a few hours off," he said
"So I brought you some firewood.

"If it don't last 'til I come again
There's that big snag up the draw
While you go to town for groceries,
I'll sharpen the axe and saw.

"Don't be too long old girl,
I have to get back tonight
The boss wants us saddled up and gone
Before first light."

So she goes to town and hurries back
Hopin' for a hug or two
It has been almost three weeks
And some lovin' is overdue!

But when she carries the groceries in
He says, "Where are my clean clothes?
And haven't you darned my favorite socks?
These all seem to have holes!"

She follows him out as he heads for the truck
With a box of clean Levis and shirts
And she's beginning to think all men on earth
Are just great big jerks!

Continued . . .

But then he takes her in his arms
And says, "Hon, I wish I could stay
Give the kids a big hug for me
And be good while I'm away

"Oh, by the way, while you're killin' time
Look for that big-titted cow
I saw her a couple of months ago
And she should have calved by now.

"Sometimes her calf can't suck
So you'll have to bring her home
And milk her out for a week or two
'Til the calf takes it on his own.

"Sorry I don't have time to shoe a horse,
I know they're all past due
All the stuff you need is in the shed,
I know you can tack on a shoe.

"Don't work too hard," he says with a smile
"I'll be back before too long
Just don't get into trouble,
Don't let anything go wrong.

"We'll be debt free in twenty years,
And then we can take it easy.
I hope you keep from getting bored,
Find enough to keep you busy."

So, there he goes in a cloud of dust,
Her man, her only love
He's not perfect, but he's all hers
And she thanks God above.

She knows that he will have to return,
He has to get his socks.
Accidentally on purpose,
She forgot to put them in his box.

TOMBOY

Dee Strickland-Johnson

I was raised with seven brothers
Near a place called Concho Lake;
There was Jamie, Jeff and Joseph
Sam and Set and Sid and Jake.
So I grew up rough and tumble,
And I made my share of noise
Romped the dogs and roped the horses,
I was rowdy as the boys!

Skinny tomboy, seven brothers,
And assorted brothers' friends
On our little cattle ponies
Raced to hell and back again.
We'd roar down the dry arroyas,
Then we'd all come tearing back.
There was Buzz and Paul and Donnie
And that rascal Charlie Black.

But one spring as I grew older,
Mama firmly told me, "No!"
And when the boys went out on roundup,
Mama said I couldn't go.
Then she tried to teach me cooking,
How to sew and keep the place,
But my heart was chasing yearlings,
And I longed to barrel race.

Once she washed my hair in soap weed.
While it still hung limp and damp,
She stuck that rusty curling iron
Down the chimney of the lamp.
"Sister," she said, holding up a gingham
Dress that she had sewed,
"Andy's comin'! Now you wear this,
So's your legs won't look so bowed."

Andy was the new young foreman
Of the ranch off to our west,
And of all my brothers' cronies
Mama showed she liked him best.
Oh, she was proud that she had made me
Look like something of a girl,
Got me out of faded Levis,
Forced my stubborn hair to curl.

Well, it wasn't long thereafter
Every time that Andy'd call,
And the boys were pitchin' horseshoes,
Andy'd linger in the hall.
So he came to be my suitor,
Brought me candy, flowers and such,
And the night he brought me perfume
Well . . . I didn't mind too much.

Andy'd come most every evening.
He was courteous and kind,
And it wasn't any secret
What that cowboy had in mind.
Every Friday we'd go dancing
Laughing clear to town and back.
Andy made me feel a lady—
So I married Charlie Black!

DADDY'S SPURS

Suzi Killman

Thank you for the compliment
I'm glad you admire my spurs
Yes, Sir, they're pretty old
And Crocketts . . . that's for sure
No, Sir, they're not for sale,
And money couldn't buy
The happy years and memories
That they have locked inside!
These old spurs whisper to me
Of a very special time
When my Dad wore them as he rode,
And I followed along behind.
He wore these old spurs many a mile
On good horses and broncs alike
They helped to hold him on in a storm
And helped him in a tight.
I recall that 'Yella horse he rode
Only had her a short spell
That ol' sow would work just fine
Then suddenly go to hell.
She'd bog her head and go to buckin'
Bawlin' with every stride
Dad would let out a war-whoop
With these spurs he'd massage her sides.
I used to listen to them jingle
In the evening after I'd gone to bed
He'd come in late after dark,
When all the stock was fed.
Where he ever got these spurs,
Really, I don't know
But it's the fact that he wore them,
That makes me love 'em so.
My Dad . . . he's been gone over twenty years
Guess now you can understand
Why I put such store in these ol' spurs
They belonged to a very special man.

THE RELUCTANT COWBOY CARPENTER

Carole Jarvis

He rebuilds a stretch of old fence, good as new,
And at hangin' gates, knows just what to do.
He builds corrals from scratch, does all their repair,
He'll climb a windmill tower, and work way up there.

I see new saddle racks, so the tack room's all done.
Reinforcing on the loading chute's just begun.
With chainsaw and hammer the ranch he'll maintain,
Except for the house, which he calls MY domain.

The porch roof is sagging, my ceiling fan quit,
Two windows won't open, and the door screen is split.
A bath faucet drip, sometimes keeps me awake,
Then the drain plugs up! Gotta' find me that "snake"!

The kitchen floor gives, each time I cross it,
The couch is worn out, I'd sure like to toss it!
But the money for that, just bought a tire,
Ten bags of cement, and six rolls of barb wire!

Now Fall has arrived, and he's back in the saddle,
Ridin' each day to gather the cattle,
So his carpenter projects have been put on hold,
Which suits him just fine, if the truth be told.

Well, I saw a two-by-four out in the woodpile,
I'll prop that porch roof; prob'ly do for a while.
And find some washers, try and stop that dang drip,
Duct tape the screen, and patch up the rip.

I don't need the fan, Autumn is here,
So those windows can stay shut, least 'til next year.
Maybe then that cowboy will do MY repair.
Who am I kidding? *I don't have a prayer!*

THUNDERSTORM

Joette Conley-Trombi

The dust-storm creeps across the desert
With boiling dust and sand.
A prelude to a cloud-burst
To quench this sun-baked land

The brown horizon looks foreboding
To other folks no doubt
The answer to a cowman's prayer
An ending to the drought.

Everything within its path
Is whipped unmercif'ly
The churning sea of brown engulfs
Each cactus, bush and tree.

Yielding to this violent beating
They bend, sway and break
When this blinding storm subsides
The desert trembles in its wake

Then thunder heads start rollin' in
Our eyes are skyward bound.
Searching for a miracle,
Precious rain upon the ground.

The thunder starts to rumble
Across that dry parched desert floor,
Like some giant mumblin'
A promise to restore.

The grass and feed the cattle need,
A cowman's main desire.
The lightning rips a jagged path
That sets the sky on fire.

Each crash and bang a symphony,
Hearts quicken to the sound.
The gentle patter of raindrops
That fall upon the ground.

The desert smell of greasewood,
Paloverde and Mesquite
There's never been a perfume
That smells half as sweet.

Like some invisible plug's been pulled
From a heavenly drain,
The blackened sky opens up,
A down pour of blessed rain.

In torrid sheets it starts to fall,
The desert drinks its fill
Dry washes turn to raging rivers
Their banks begin to spill.

Normal folks would stay indoors
Protected, safe and dry.
Cowmen climb in their pickup trucks,
Some people wonder why.

We've got to see the washes run,
See if the stock tanks fill
Our livelihood depends on rain,
That's why it's such a thrill.

Each cowman is a gambler,
Who lives on faith alone.
With each thunderstorm,
God's omnipotence we're shown.

Nature's violent reminder,
Just in case we forgot.
It's like playing the lottery,
And we've just hit the jackpot.

HOME COMING RAIN

Carrol Williams

Thunder in the mountains,
     Lord, how we hope it rains.
The pregnant clouds, black and low,
     are held back by mountain chains.

Everyday we are watching, hoping to
     see them come down.
Oh, by the way we heard it rained
     up at Prescott town.

Jump over the mountain fences.
     Slide down the canyons deep.
Please dear rain keep coming,
     all the trees begin to weep.

A ha! The bolt of lightning
     hits the hard dry ground;
Close, almost in our house,
     thunder makes its cannon sound.

We see a trickle of water
     come down the Hassayamp.
It's coming from the north
     down from the Bradshaw camp.

The Hassayampa has been so dry
     at least three months or so.
It's running muddy water now.
     Would you listen to it flow!

We can smell the rain. It's coming.
     The air gets hot and still;
And soon we hear the rain drops
     fall on the window sill.

Another thunder crashes
    and all the dogs run to the porch.
We can smell the Ozone
    where the lightning bolt has scorched.

Coming down now in buckets,
    we can't see across the yard.
Water is running fast in gushes.
    it's really raining hard.

We look into each other's eyes,
    as we, too, sit on the porch.
We see rivers running down our faces,
    that have been so long sun scorched.

RANCH MANAGER'S CHRISTMAS

Carol Malnar

The boys are gettin' restless
Now that the season is on hand
They're paging through the catalogs
With a list to beat the band.

We're puttin' up the wreaths and bells
Santa Fe candles in paper bags
The place is lookin' cheerful
Like Cinderelly steppin' out of her rags.

We're workin' a few odd jobs
For a little extra dough
Seems Christmas is right expensive
As you all probably know.

The company's havin' a party
It's three hundred miles away
Reckon we ain't gonna make it
There'd be nobody to throw the hay!

Pa said we'd go to Flagstaff
To shop for boots and coats
Our truck is runnin' poorly
It near ran out of oats.

Our little house ain't no bigger
As we was hopin' it would be
We're packed in mighty cozy
The boys 'n' dad and me.

It's so dern cold out
All the cats are comin' in
They take up all the chairs and couch
There's usually 'bout ten.

Yep, we're gettin' in the spirit
The bank account is low
We'll be eatin' a lot more beans
And now it's gonna' snow!

WHAT REALLY MATTERED

Lola Chiantaretto

My heroes have mostly been cowboys
Listening to their stories is one of life's joys.
I admired their ways and tack,
But there was one thing that I thought they lacked.

Most of the cowpunchers that I admired
Had hats I'd like to throw into the fire.
So, it was my earnest goal
To keep my hat as black as coal.

Every day or maybe two,
I'd clean it up and restore its hue.
Round up time came 'round
Those cows and calves had to be found.

The days could last into the night
My mind was on cattle and how to do the job right.
We'd come in from workin' those cows
"I'll clean it tomorrow," faithfully I'd vow.

Fall turned to winter and winter into spring
With it a new perspective and respect it did bring.
For in the time that had passed
I learned a lesson from the working cowboy class.

You see, my hat is now dirty and wore,
Just like the cowpuncher's I mentioned before.
Instead of worrying about the dirt on my hat
I'm more concerned about the cows and where they were at.

Now when I see a hat that's dirty and tattered,
I know it belongs to someone
Who knows what *really mattered!*

ROANIE

Mary Abbott

My good horse is thirteen this year
Gosh, that's hard to savvy
Been together eleven good years
He's boss horse of the cavvy.

There's no better horse through rock and brush
Just knows where to put his feet
For crawling up through the toughest slopes
Being safe he can't be beat.

He'll still snort at the saddling time
Can take a hard day in stride
He's stout and fit and tough as they come
Still strong at the end of the ride.

I've got more good horses in my string
As it comes they get their turn
Long hours, big circles go to colts
'Cause they've got lots more to learn.

When Roanie is on the back burner
Loafing at rest in the shade
Others get the wet saddle blankets
That's how good horses are made.

But let a tough ride come into view
Where I might have lots to lose,
As my mind's eye runs through my horses,
It's Roanie's bridle I'll choose.

CHANGING TIMES

Bertha Monroe

There's time to think while on horseback
It's refreshing to get out in the hills
Where life's fast pace slows way down
It's a life without many "frills".

I was riding along just thinking about
How the environmentalists want to take
This stream of water and that tree there,
And more area for some bird's sake.

They claim the cattle pollute the streams
And leave cowpies all over the land
Don't they know that water gets purified
As it runs through rocks and sand?

As for the cowpies, they melt with rain,
And provide fertilizer for the grasses
You'd almost think God planned it that way
To keep a balance in "nature's" masses!

If the rains do come in Arizona
The grass grows and streams run clear
And it's not those biodiversified dudes
That's protecting our land so dear.

God's the one in charge of the land
And we ranchers are stewards He chose,
And do much more to maintain wild life
Than the environmentalist even knows.

They get their information out of books
Written by another of the same,
We get ours from living with the land,
To preserve it was always our aim

Time marches on and things do change
"Progress" doesn't delight me at all
The "city boys" blame it all on the cattle
But in truth it's the big urban sprawl.

HAIL AND FAREWELL

Delia Gardner

Think not on my brittle bones mingling with dust
They're but a handful added to those gone before
Think rather that on this borrowed hilltop
One lived joyously and died content.
In this dark soil I found reminders
Saying, "You too will pass;
Savor for us the wind and the sun."
From smoke blackened earth I dug a frail shell bracelet
Shaped skillfully, lovingly, for a brown-skin wrist now dust
That piece of broken clay was a doll's foot and leg
Artfully curved, made for a brown eyed child.
Pottery shards sayin' "Yours for a little time only,
Take delight in this as we did."
The tree will die, the vine'll wither and rattle in the wind
For I broke a law of nature
I carried water to the hilltop.
Nevertheless,
For those that follow there will be these things I've loved.
Morning sun rays
Slanting across the great trees in the green meadow.
Wind.
The great blue sky.
Peace of the encircling hills,
And the flaming glow of sunset.

The Men:
Neighboring
Poets

1991 Poster Artwork   by Shawn Cameron

A CAMP MAN'S DAY

Ray Fitzgerald

He's up before dawn and his lantern is lit
He's done fed his horse and he'll eat in a bit

He's already drinkin' coffee it's time to turn the steak
The biscuits are brownin' and some gravy he'll make.

He's finished his breakfast, and the dishes are done
He heads for the corral— now there may be some fun

The horse he's kept up is still plenty green
Some mornin's he'll buck but he ain't really mean.

He was raised on the range, for five years he ran free
Now he's learnin' new ways but it's stranage, don't you see?

The rider's a good hand and this bronc he respects
For this big hearted pony gives him all he expects.

He saddles the horse then leads him outside
He steps in the saddle and he's ready to ride

The horse bucks a few jumps, but it's sorta' half-hearted
Then he brings his head up and a new day has started

They head for a tank the man knows is near dry
They move all the cows to another nearby

They get to the new tank along about four
When the calves mother up it's too late to do more.

But there's no cause to worry it's been a good day
They done what they could and each earned his pay.

Continued . . .

He brings in the cavvy as he comes through the trap
When he gets them all grained he's on the last lap

He turns 'em all out except for just one
Then heads for the cabin, the day's nearly done

He cooks him some supper then cleans up his shack
Rolls into his bunk as the night turns to black.

Artwork by Mike Capron

FEAR

Larry McWhorter

I've been on the mountain and been on the plain
When lightning was casting its lot.
It isn't much fun having nowhere to run
When the sulphur is heavy and hot.

Been wrapped in my rope without prayer or hope,
Thinking, "Maybe I should learn to dally."
My foot in the stirrup, stuck hard like dried syrup
Knowing God has just totaled my tally.

Been knocked down and wooled around by a bull.
Had cows bounce me off of a fence.
There's plenty to fear, day to day, year to year
If a cowboy has got any sense.

I've felt my blood chill through wreck and through spill.
Cold sweat has poured off of my head.
I've felt my heart sink if I had time to think
On dangers I knew lay ahead.

Yet fear we must face having chosen our place
Knowing full well this life ain't all clover.
We're knocked down but then we get up again
And try to laugh when it's over.

But there is one trap that gets dropped in our lap,
Each man has to face on his own.
You just can't prepare for this worst kind of scare
And you'll never feel so all alone

As when out of the blue, directed at you,
These words that make men hunt their hat.
"I got it on sale, but I really can't tell,
Does this outfit make me look fat?"

HEAVEN SCENT

Ken Graydon

There's folks who will tell you that nothing compares
To a garden of roses in spring
Others maintain that freshly baked bread
Has a fragrance that's fit for a king.
There's some like the odor of leather
Of saddles and harness and tack
Or a fresh cut pine board on a hot summer day
When you're patching the walls of a shack.
There's some like the smell of the ocean
When it rolls on the shore in a storm
Or the star jasmine's scent at the end of the day
When the evening is gentle and warm.
But ask any rancher and he'll tell you straight out
That to him it is perfectly plain
That of all life's perfumes, the sweetest by far,
Is the first fifteen minutes of rain.

THE SNUBBIN' POST. . . *or Silent Witness*

Mike Prince

An old cowman leaned against the fence
And gazed across the pen
At a lone and scarred old snubbin' post
And his thoughts went back to when
    They were both young.

Tall and straight you were, old post,
When first we planted you
In the middle of this old bronc pen
Tall and straight was I then too,
    For we were both young.

You were clear pine, stout, unyeilding
I was a boy becoming a man
Full of dash and daring and love of life
A wild and wooly ranahan.
    Course . . . I was young then.

I roped the broncs, you held my dallies
As war raged 'tween man and brute
Wild-eyed broncos and reckless young waddies
Ah, but wasn't life a hoot?
    Shore! We were young then!

You remember that bronc the boys ran in
From off the 2 Bar Y?
The black with the droopy lower lip,
And the dead fish look in his eye?
And how the old man asked me not to crawl him?
    But I did . . . 'cause I was young then.

Continued . . .

An' I thought I could ride anything with hair
The boys, they all thought so too.
And how they cheered when I raised the blinds
And gave the black his cue.
　　　Ah, the boys . . . they were so young then.

The black horse changed my life that day
When he bucked into the fence
And ran that pine stob clean through my leg
But, you saw it, and in his defense,
　　　Well . . . he was young then too.

The old cowman paused in his silent thoughts
And then, in a voice checked by age,
He said, "Old friend, I sure miss them broncs
And the battles we used to wage . . .
　　　Back when we were young."

Then he grinned, "You're shorter now, and so am I
And our scars they sure run deep.
We're both a lookin' plumb tired and worn,
But we've memories, a heap.
　　　Now that we're not young.

Then the old cowman pulled his hat down low
As the sun set in the West
And he bid adieu to the silent witness
And the days they loved the best . . .
　　　Back when they were young.

THE HORSEMAN

Gary Robertson

I was standin' by the fire
As the sky was turnin' grey.
'Twas the hour before the sunrise
The coldest time of day.

He walked up with his hat in hand
As I stood there all alone
Said, "Boss, I hate to say it,
But I'm chilled right to the bone.

"I never knew I could be so cold
Or could ever hurt so bad
An' I'm wonderin' why I ever left
My mother 'n' my dad."

He was somethin' short-a sixteen then
Had just hired on with the brand
But I knew he had the heart 'n' mind
To make a first-rate hand.

See, he sat natural in the saddle
Was firm, yet gentle with the rein
He'd ride any mount you gave him
An' he weren't one to complain.

I poured us both some coffee
Handed him his cup
An' we stood there without talkin'
As we watched the sun come up.

That eastern sky turned light, then bright,
Then exploded into day
It was while we watched that sunrise
I decided what I'd say.

Continued . . .

I said, "You've got to feel the bitter cold,
To see the day's first light,
An' you've got to sleep out on the ground,
To touch the stars, at night.

"An' you've got to live life lonely,
To cherish kith 'n' kin,
It's livin' as you're meant to live,
That comforts in the end.

"You were meant to live life horseback.
I've known it from the start.
Why, the first time that you climbed aboard
The Good Lord touched your heart.

"An' it's God who picks the Horseman
It ain't us fellers who decide.
See, it's 'need' not 'want' that drives us
To live so's we can ride.

"Oh, you're a Horseman now, He's made that plain,
You're one of the proud 'n' the few,
An' the way you live, it's who you are,
It's not just what you do.

"There's no goin' back to Mom 'n' Dad,
You can't return to pushin' plow,
For you've seen the world from horseback,
You're a Horseman, like us, now.

"We ain't built like other fellers,
We're cursed as much as blessed,
For once we've forked a saddle,
We can't live like all the rest.

"Once we've smelled them lathered horses,
An', a wood-fed brandin' fire,
We're hooked on workin' horseback.
An' we'll live our life bone-tired."

"We'll put up with the heat 'n' dust,
Or the ice 'n' freezin' cold,
An' we know that long before our time,
This life will make us old.

"But we take the cards life deals us,
And we gladly play that hand,
Cause, when you're sittin' horseback, son,
You don't look up, to any man."

TO CHOOSE A HERO

Leon Autrey

He came back from World War II, in 1945
Shot up in the war, was just glad to survive
Three years of healing before he could come home
Walking on a wooden leg, his real one was gone
He would ride a horse, or climb a windmill
Flank big calves, he had determination and will

I've seen him in awful pain
But he would keep working, never complain
I've seen him dig post holes, and build a corral
I've seen him rope and doctor a wild eyed cow
I've worked right beside him as a boy and a man
He taught me to love and appreciate this great Land

This Great American is a Hero to me
He's grown old now, and slowed with time
And if I were to choose a Hero
HE WOULD BE MINE

THE ROUND CORRAL

Tom Sharpe

Down in Southern Colorado where the foothills meet the plains,
Where the mesas run on eastward, and it seldom ever rains,
A mile above the Purgatoire, full of history and ghosts,
There's a round corral of lodgepole and crooked cedar posts.

It was Dad and I who built it, back when I was only 10,
Posts were tamped in solid, poles laid high made up the pen.
The ground was smoothed and leveled where it cut into the grade
And a giant cottonwood would lend its cooling shade.

I spent a lot of time there when I was young and green
Ridin' horses owned by others, turned out to be routine.
It became my place of refuge, to let my feelings out,
An escape from what I lived with, all the fear and doubt.

At first, when I was little, and found myself inside,
Two half welsh ponies, small and brown, were set for me to ride.
It took a lot of schoolin', for I was young and didn't know,
So a hired hand would help me, to make those ponies go.

Dad would sometimes be there, with his rough and tumble ways,
Pushin', laughin', cussin', but he found no way to praise.
I only sought approval, just to ride those horses right,
But he had a way to scare me, 'til I couldn't sleep at night.

It never seemed to matter how well I rode a colt,
Dad would always spook him, make him buck or bolt.
He'd laugh when I got dusted, said I'd never make a hand,
My spirit soon was busted, for I didn't understand.

It was his way of teachin' me, trying to make me tough,
What he did, didn't work. He played the game too rough.
But still I kept on ridin' 'um, learnin' as I went
With bigger, tougher horses, until my youth was spent.

Continued . . .

I found that I could handle it, when I was left alone.
When someone offered help, it would gravel to the bone.
My anger and resentment ran deep back in those days,
I couldn't see reality, I was running in a maze.

That solid old pine round corral became my hiding place,
Where no one saw the many tears go running down my face.
I lost the fear, my anger flared, then I didn't care,
Any horse would suit me fine, as long as I was there.

I grew careless with what I rode, what I'd say and do,
My life had lost its meaning, and everybody knew.
Being old enough by then, to light out on my own,
I packed my truck with anger, and headed off alone.

Miles and camps and cattle took me far from home,
Figured life would turn out good, if I'd only roam.
But trouble was my partner and he wouldn't go away.
I drifted back to the round corral, hopin' I could stay.

It was unchanged, wouldn't work, felt I'd lost my mind,
A better way to spend my days is what I had to find.
Lookin' deep within myself, at resentment, anger, fear,
Why the troubles followed me, soon came crystal clear.

A higher stronger round corral was built inside of me,
It kept my feelings locked away where no one else could see.
When the gate was opened up, all these things came out,
I rode them hard, one by one, anger, fear and doubt.

A better life is what I made, the world is still unchanged,
A bitter kid is more content, matured and rearranged.
Years have taken youth from me, this I don't regret.
If it wasn't such a rugged trail, I wouldn't be here yet.

Someday, perhaps, my son and I can build a round corral,
Then we'll spend some time in there, he'll be my special pal,
I'd tell him of so many things, like troubles that I had,
And hopefully the trail he rides, is smoothed some by his Dad.

DAY'S END

Jim Shelton

The sun is nearly down
And our day is nearly through
You spent your day for me
And I spent my day with you
Now the campsite, we can see it
In the valley down below
I pat your tired neck
And pard we'll take it slow
The sweat on you is dryin'
And you'll get rest tonight
Your turn don't come for four more days
Old horse you did alright.

A BETTER JOB

Ride up a little faster, boys,
I've dropped out of the drive
And won't be there for breakfast
When ol' cooky calls at five.

Don't bring no long, sad faces
When you lay me in the ground
For I'll be through with calvin' jobs
And pore cows that are down.

Just think of roundups, we have made,
With all the fun we had
A ridin' horses good and true
And some few that were bad.

We've not spoke of religion much,
But anyone could see
The handiwork of God
In baby calves a runnin' free.

I put my faith in Jesus Christ,
Some few years in the past
And didn't worry none about
How long this life would last.

So 'member all the good times,
And know that where I'm at
The horses all are gentle,
And the cattle always fat.

THE AUCTION BARN CAFÉ

Don Cadden

Old men sit in overalls, coffee cups at hand
Hats and caps at the jaunty tilt, that identifies the man
Dominos and playing cards start another day
It's the early morning ritual, down at the Auction Barn Café

The hands that deal the cards are big
The rough and callused kind
It was to the land they gave their work
With honest heart and mind

Maybe they were farmers, a lifetime working soil
A family and a way of life built on sweat and toil
Or maybe they were ranchers, that knew the cowboy way
Now they tell of the broncs they rode,
    down at the Auction Barn Café

Each day's a bit more precious now
Their sunset's drawing near
So they meet their pards and they share a cup
And they bend each other's ear

Some men sit in boardrooms
Money and power make their day
But pray we always have men like those
Down at the Auction Barn Café.

CODE

By Leon Flick

I learned my way with cattle,
   from the men full wise to battle,
They used snaffle bit, and hackamore, and spade
They were eager, brass, and bold,
   as were the stories that they told.
And also were the horses that they made.

They sang a tune to leather creakin'
   and their spur rowels softly speakin'
As their horses trotted rhythm in the sage
They were horse of leg and bone
   that could trot a man back home
After thirty miles behind them on a voyage.

Men of cowboy rules
   from the old vaquero schools
Each man rode his spot based on position
If it was on your side
   that's the country you would ride
It was expected of all without exception

You never crossed in front,
   and you seldom crossed behind
And if you did, it was with social graces
You held the spot that you'd been given
   and there wasn't much forgiven
With men who were always tradin' places

You went out there as a team
   and you made your plans and schemes
But it was still the cow that cut the final deal
Where and how, is what she'd tell
   and she'd blow your plans to - - - -
Well, a good crew just adjusted to the feel.

Every person packed a knife
　　that you trusted with your life
And you hoped that they could reach you if need be
Cuz if you got fowled and tied
　　to some spooked and kickin' snide
Your pardner's all that saved eternity

You trusted one another
　　and you counted on the other
To take up slack, or give a little room
Cuz your life depended on it
　　and your pardners in this sonnet
Like as not, are like some sitting in this room

Men of plenty savvy
　　and their horses in the cavvy
Were just as much a measure of their pride
Their string of horses— theirs alone
　　to ride another man's unknown
Unless the deal'd been made before the ride

They gave their colts the time they needed
　　subtle cues and lessons heeded
Wasn't long before they gave their heart and try
Gentle hands of give and take
　　trying always not to break
The spirit that would pack them till they'd die

They strung their cows like siphoned water
　　and a feller knew he oughta
Keep the sides tucked in, and leave the drag alone
Cuz if you push and pound
　　it'll only slow you down
And it won't be long till baby calves "go home"

Oh, those days of brush and saddle
　　as you tended to the cattle
How it felt as you all trotted as "one crew"
Out on some sagebrush range
　　far away from strife and change
Give me five good colts and let me "buckaroo".

WHEN HORSES TALK WAR
THERE'S SMALL CHANCE FOR PEACE

Mike Logan

Charlie Russell left this tableau
Of the old time cow camp way
When men was up and saddled
Before the break of day.

This bronc's a makin' war talk.
Blowin' rollers t' the sky.
There ain't one sign of peaceful
In that ol' roan's wicked eye.

Ol' Bob's a standin' easy.
While he ain't bent on war,
Way he's holdin' that McCarty tells
They've had this talk before.

He's workin' on his mornin' smoke.
His fish is tied plumb loose.
Ain't makin' one concession
T' no cold backed roan cayuse.

The roan's all bunched an' goosey.
He's proddy 'n' some tough.
His medicine's plumb potent
An' his war talk ain't no bluff.

First light it's just a showin'
Dawn's comin' cold an' damp.
Looks like ol' Bob an' Roanie's
Gonna entertain the camp.

A RARE FIND

Randy Rieman

It's a wonderful thing
    somewhat hard to explain
        when you meet a new friend on your way.
You know in no time
    there's a reason behind
        the ease that the friendship obtained.
For your spirits are one,
    though the friendship begun
        only just a few hours ago.
The things that you share
    and the feeling that's there
        is more lasting and precious than gold.
Your talk runs from horses
    to shoeing to cattle
        to startin' these colts a good way.
But before your own eyes
    the time has flown by
        adios is the thing you now say.
You sure hate to go
    your feelings show on your face
        as you shake your friend's hand.
Yet you know that you're blessed
    to have this new friend
        who shares your same love for the land.
For horses and cattle
    for days in the saddle
        for nights underneath a clear sky.
A sameness in spirit
    that goes beyond words,
        we share that my new friend and I.
As I lift up my head
    from my old canvas bed
        I thank the good Lord for His care,

And for my new friend
hope we'll soon meet again
for I know we have much more to share.
For our spirits are one,
though our friendship begun
only just a few hours ago.
The things that we share
and the feeling that's there
is more lasting and precious than gold.

1990 Poster Artwork   by Mark Billington

LET'S SHOOT ONE OR THE OTHER

Paul Schmitt

The crew is awful quiet
No one is sayin' a word
The clangin' of the head catch
Is the only sound that's heard.

Then the squeeze is pulled tight—
And all hell breaks loose for sure;
Roger the preg. tester with gloved arm
Is checkin' her.

I'm sure you have known of a cow like this,
She's always on the fight
She can spot a rider half mile away
And that's when she takes to flight.

To the farthest corner of the ranch—
She can run just like a deer.
It took the whole durn crew all day
Just to get her into here.

But when you get her in the corral
The battle's only half won.
She can fold up a Powder River gate
Just like an accordion.

The bravest hand will clear the top rail,
The dogs all head for the truck
This old sister is out for blood
And she's runnin' plumb amuck.

But she weans a big calf every year!
The boss won't sell a cow like that.
Ain't got a tooth left in her head
But she's always rollin' fat.

Continued . . .

101

So we're hopin' she'll be open
That ornery, bunch quittin' cuss.
She's got to be at least fifteen,
Been here longer than any of us!

We're all standin' there a wishin'
That she's run out of luck
It'd be like Christmas, your birthday,
And the Fourth of July
Just to see her in that truck!

Now Roger calls out to the crew -
And Roger's never wrong
*"Turn her in with the keepers, boys,
'Cause she's six months along."*

HORSE WHISPERERS

Wally McRae

Tom Dorance got it started, down in Californ I A
Then Ray Hunt latched onto it, and made the dang thing pay
As gunsels, dudes and youngsters, and lonely single ladies
Genuflected in the sawdust to evade the fires of Hades.
Then Redford made a movie that gave the movement mass
And clueless horseman caught the fever,
> *"And lo, it came to pass"*

That the Horse Whisperer Religion, from Beaumont to Calgary
Swept across the landscape, until it reached epiphany.

Some baptized in the round corral,
> who declared themselves devout,

Were the folks whose saddle pads
> were never wet from inside out.

These new converts to the movement began to testify
That any non-believer was fair game to vility.
"Make the right thing pleasant." "Get inside the horse's head."
Like lambs condemned for slaughter,
> we were haltered up and led.

Reluctance was rejected. Second guesses were ignored.
Sometimes they even prayed for us
> to the "Horse Whispering Lord."

Their disciples were seductive like Nabokov's "Lolita."
"The horse is always right?" I'd ask,
"Sounds like something posed by PETA."
"Your horse is in the wrong lead!" they holler and they grin,
"You turned that cow, old timer, but committed mortal sin."
"To each his own, I'll shut my trap," I thought
> *"I've had enough."*

But my critics were not satisfied, they'd ask to call my bluff,
"Are you a true believer? Have you been sanctified?"
I bit my lip. I hemmed and hawed. I might as well have lied.

Continued . . .

So now I ride with horsemen, as if in a pleasure class
Their horses all are happy, but what grates my pancreas
Is we just aren't COWBOYING. The job's not getting done.
No one wants to turn that steer who's vamoosing on the run.
No one wants to mash a beast while carving up a herd.
They hang back until their "horsie"
    finally whispers *them* the word.
So the more I ride with horsemen, the more I understand
That, *a horseman is a horseman, but a cowboy makes a hand!*

RITE OF PASSAGE

Jesse Smith

You've been out with the wagon,
Spent your share of time in camp.
You've never been nobody's hero,
Never been some big world champ.

In fact, you're just a cowboy
Out in your part of the West.
You make your livin' horseback,
'Cause that's what you like to do the best.

Some say it's an addiction,
Bad as any booze or dope,
But this addiction revolves around
A horse, a cow, a rope.

Some say, "Oh, how romantic."
Now me, you've got to show
The romanticism in it
When it's zero, or below.

And you're a long ways from camp
And you can't feel your toes,
And you've got this great big icicle
Danglin' underneath your nose.

Or when it's hot and dusty
And you can't see or breathe
The boss man ain't around to quit
And you just can't up and leave.

'Cause you gotta wait 'till payday
Of that, there's little doubt.
Payday comes, you still can't leave
After they hold your taxes out.

Continued . . .

Or when they lead you out a horse
You know it's your bad luck,
And you can see with one eye
This old pony's gonna buck.

But you throw your saddle on him,
Throw caution to the wind.
About the time you slam the ground,
You get your caution back again.

You lay there a-gaspin'
Tryin' hard to catch your breath.
The world around you teeters,
You feel that awful clutch of death.

But you know that you ain't dyin'
When you hear some damned fool say,
As he comes trottin' up,
"Hey, pard, are you okay?"

Or when the rain's a-pourin' down
And your hat dye streaks your face,
And the cattle that you're tryin to move
Move along at a turtle pace.

You think about your cabin
With the stove so nice and warm,
And your horse and cattle turn their heads,
Tryin' not to face the storm.

For when you got a camp job
And the holidays come 'round,
You know you'll spend them all alone
'Cuz you're far from home and town.

You think it's just another day
But when that day begins,
Though you tried hard not to think about it,
Loneliness sets in.

Now you're gettin' old
And your hair's a turnin' gray
But you think back with fond memories
Of all the yesterdays.

You've never made a fortune,
And you've never gained no fame
But you've earned the right to have "Cowboy"
Written right beside your name.

RIDIN' HER

Hook Hill

It was rough going, up there, as tough as could be.
Hang on for dear life and await the decree.
Could I ride this sidewinder going down and around?
Seemed more likely to me I'd soon hit the ground.

I'd been checking the cattle in country real wild,
Ridin' gently along like an innocent child.
We started down a mean hill and things came unglued.
I felt like a beginner, a green eastern dude.

I'd been a bronc buster for near twenty years
But ridin' this critter taught me some new fears.
Crawfishin' don't tell it and whirlin' won't do,
The moves comin' at me were totally new.

My neck got snapped back, I bit my tongue 'til it bled,
My ears were both ringin' 'til it was splittin' my head.
The dust was a flyin' so I couldn't see much, but
We'd soon know how this hombre would react in a clutch.

I dug in with my spurs, hung on with both hands,
Lost my new Stetson, saw it roll o'er the lands.
I heard a weird noise comin' from the dust cloud,
Then I realized it was me; I was screamin' out loud.

Of a sudden, it was over; we came to a stop.
I was one surprised hombre . . . still up there on top.
I've ridden wild horses of all sizes and shapes,
But nothin' I've seen. . . beats a Ford pickup with no brakes!

FOR WOODY

Rod McQueary

From the snowdrifts in the canyons,
    behind the granite and the pinion,
Past the trout and beaver,
    where young quakies crowd to share,
From the icy plaster caked across
    the mountain goat's dominion,
Comes the lifeblood of our valley,
    as it tumbles down from there.

And it gurgles, almost chuckles
    past the boulders, and the gravel,
Cheerfully, it detours
    through the ditches man might make.
With only gravity— its master,
    it always knows which way to travel,
Warm and foamy, ever downward,
    through the sloughs toward the lake.

There, the bullrush stops the riffles,
    where the sheets of ice lay dying.
The waxing sun shows promise
    the winter's lost its sting.
Overhead, the floating regiments
    of geese formations, flying,
Driven Northward, to their nesting grounds
    by instinct, every spring.

In one pasture by the water,
    tired pension horses wander.
They wait for my alfalfa,
    and the sun to conquer cold.
In this middle ground—'tween active duty,
    and the promised yonder,
They don't care too much for scenery.
    They are thin and tired and old.

Continued . . .

Last among these pensioners,
        one sorrel gelding stumbles.
With swollen knees and seedy toe,
        you see why he's so lame.
He's lost his youth, but not his dignity.
        He'll die before he humbles,
He was my Dad's top saddle horse,
        and "Woody" is his name.

I never cared for Woody;
        he's not the kind of horse I cling to.
He was hard to catch, and fussy,
        and he never made a pet,
But he could jump at cattle,
        and that is one thing he would do.
He had the heart of giants.
        I can still recall it yet.

We were bringing calvy heifers
        from a close and handy pasture.
Bus rode bronco Woody,
        'cause he had a lot to learn.
One heifer broke. They ran to head her,
        held their ground and stopped disaster.
With dewclaws cutting circles,
        they beat that cow at every turn.

So she ran blind—for the willows.
        Bus and Woody had to race her.
Nose to nose, and pushing shoulders,
        as she made this frantic try,
And they pushed her in a circle,
        till she quit, and they could face her,
Because Buster wouldn't weaken,
        and Woody did not let her by.

And now I watch him strain to shuffle.
      I touch my rifle, 'neath the seat.
It is a friend of suffering horses,
      and at this range, I couldn't miss.
He'd find green pastures in an instant.
      For my Dad, I'd do it neat.
He'd never hear the whisper,
      never feel the nosler's kiss.

But the cranes have come. They're dancing,
      as the spring sun melts the snow.
Oh, I know I'll need that rifle,
      on some cold, November day.
But for a sorrel colt
      who beat a wringy heifer, long ago,
I'll just go about my business,
      until this feeling . . . goes away.

WORDS THAT WHISPER THROUGH THE GRASS

Joel Nelson

Words that whisper through the grass
Through Piñon Pine and mountain pass
Then edge their way into my mind
In hope that I might somehow find
Some way to sort them into verse
Have cast on me the blessed curse.

Words that whisper through the grass
Through Aspen grove and deep crevasse
Come howling in on Norther' cold
And plead to have their story told .
"You must! You must!" they say to me
"Assume responsibility."

They come by ones or twos or threes
And I cannot ignore their pleas
So with compliance some begin
To flow from out my trembling pen
Like harnessed teams in perfect time
They work in meter and in rhyme.

Words that whisper sometimes shout
They must be loose and leave no doubt
They'd rather tell their story free
Of polished form and symmetry.
So I relent— the slave alas
To words that whisper through the grass.

FIRST YOU FEED YOUR HORSE

Ray Owens

A cold and blust'ry, bitter night
The boy was nearly froze
His hands were numb upon the reins,
No feelin' in his toes.
He struggled just to stay aboard
His stumblin' jaded horse
As they plowed through wind-blown, driftin' snow
But somehow kept their course.

They headed toward a beacon
Flickerin' faintly in the night
Through the howlin', swirlin', icy hell
They traveled toward the light
And the welcome, sheltered safety
Of a barn and cabin warm
Where the horse and half-froze boy could start
To thaw out from the storm.

His pa was watchin' for 'em
And he met 'em at the gate
"Your ma was gettin' worried, son
It's gettin' kinda' late.
Got some beef stew simmerin' on the stove
Fresh coffee in the pot
'Pears to me that you could prob'ly use
Some vittles nice an' hot.

"Let me help you strip that saddle off
And dry 'im off a mite
Then we'll brush 'im down a little,
Man! That blizzard is a sight!
An extra scoop of grain might help
He'll like this fresh, clean hay
A good long rest and he'll be fit
To work another day.

Continued . . .

"And son, you might be thinking' now
'Myself, I'm kinda tired!
My hands near froze, my feet like ice,
Is all this work required?'
But son, you know the custom here
Though we say it kinda coarse . . .
'Fore you back your butt up to the fire,
First you take care of your horse!

"'Ya see, he's why you're standin' here
'Steada out there in the snow.
He brought you home, safe through the storm
It weren't no easy go.
Every step he took was forward,
No balkin', no complaint
A man can claim to be well mounted,
When he's ridin' this old paint."

A lesson learned while just a youth
Still shapes his code today
A grown man now, his word's his bond,
Each day he earns his pay.
And no matter what the weather,
Or if the hour's late,
He takes care of his horse before
He goes to fill his plate.

I wonder if the world might be
A kinder, better place
If more of us embraced that code
'Steada tryin' to erase
The truths and values of our youth
And followed straight the course.
Think we'd 'preciate life more today,
If first, we'd feed our horse.

THE HORSE TRADE

Sunny Hancock

I traded for a horse one time,
He wouldn't take no beauty prize;
A great big long-geared, blue roan gelding,
Not too bad for weight or size.
I had to make some tough old circles
And this trader guaranteed
This horse would show me lots of country
And not need too much rest or feed.

He said, "Now this here ain't no kids' horse
But he'll pack you up the crick,
He will hump up on some occasions
And he has been known to kick.
I wouldn't trade him to just anyone
Without having some remorse
But if you're a sure enough cow puncher,
Mister, he's your kind of horse."

I stepped on that horse next mornin'
He began to buck and bawl
That trader maybe hadn't lied none,
But he hadn't told it all.
Because we sure tore up the country
Where he throwed that equine fit
And I almost ran out of hand holds
By the time he finally quit.

I guess that musta' set the pattern;
Things just never seemed to change,
Although I showed him lots of country,
Every corner of the range.
But every time I'd ride that booger,
Why, he'd keep me sittin' tight.
I knew I'd make at least three bronc rides
'Fore he'd pack me home that night.

Continued . . .

115

Which woulda' been ok
With lots of horses that I knowed,
But that old pony had my number;
I'd just barely get him rode.
And the thing that really spooked me
And put a damper on my pride
Was he was learning how to buck
Faster'n I was learnin' how to ride.

I pulled into camp one evening;
It was gettin' pretty late
I see this grey horse in the corral
And there's a saddle by the gate.
I looked that grey horse over
And I sure liked what I seen,
Then this kid showed up around the barn;
He musta' been about sixteen.

He said he'd lamed the grey that morning
Coming down off granite grade,
And he wondered if I had a horse
I'd maybe like to trade.
He said he didn't have time to stop
And rest and let him heal,
And since that beggars can't be choosers,
He'd make most any kind of deal.

When a feller's tradin' hosses,
Why most anything is fair,
So I traded him that blue roan
For his grey horse then and there.
But then my conscience started hurtin'
When I thought of what I did,
To trade a "fly blown dink" like that
Off to some wet-nosed kid.

So next mornin' after breakfast,
Why, I tells him, "Listen, lad,
If you want to know the truth,
That trade you made last night was bad.

That old blue horse is a tough one,
Bad as any one you'll see.
He'll kick you, strike you, stampede.
He's a sorry S.O.B.

"It's all I can do to ride him
And I'll tell it to you straight,
I think you'll be awfully lucky
Just to ride him past the gate.
There's two or three old horses
Out there in the saddle bunch
They ain't got too much goin' for 'em
But I kinda' got a hunch

"They'll probably get you where you're going
If you just don't crowd 'em none,
But, damn, I hate to see you ride
That blue roan booger, son!"
He said, "I told you there last night
I'd make most any kind of trade,
And I appreciate your tellin'
What a bad mistake I made.

"But my old daddy told me when you're tradin'
That no matter how you feel,
Even if you take a whippin'
That a deal is still a deal.
That horse, you say has lots of travel,
And he's not too bad for speed.
Well, sir, I'm kinda' in a tight
And that's exactly what I need.

"I traded for him fair and square
And damn his blue roan hide,
When I pull outta' here this morning,
That's the horse I'm gonna' ride."
I watched him cinching up his saddle
And he pulled his hat way down,
Stepped right up into the riggin'
Like he's headed straight for town.

Continued . . .

Stuck both spurs up in his shoulders,
Got the blue roan hair a-flyin'
Tipped his head straight back and screamed
Just like a hungry mountain lion.
You know, I've heard a lot of stories
'Bout the bucking horse ballet,
I've heard of poetry in motion,
But the ride I saw that day

Just plumb complete defied description
Though I still can see it plain
Like it happened in slow motion
And was branded on my brain.
I don't suppose I could explain it
To you even if I tried.
The only thing that I can say is,
By the Saints, that kid could ride!

He sat there plumb relaxed
Like he was laying home in bed,
And every jump that pony made,
That kid's a-half a jump ahead.
When it was over I decided
I could learn a few things still,
And I said, "Son, I'm awfully sorry
I misjudged your ridin' skills."

He just said, "Shucks, that's OK, mister,"
As he started on his way,
"But if you think this horse can buck,
Don't put your saddle on that grey."

LESSONS

Dan Schmitt

One thousand-seven games of rummy were played
Beneath the shade
Of our modern-day chuckwagon,
A broke down trailer truck.
So skillfully each hand was dealt,
So cautious was it played
The winner voiced his victory
And the losers cursed bad luck.

Then later,
After supper, our evening hours were lost
Shoeing horses, roping bushes and reading western books
Taking turns at telling stories
Taking rough looks from the boss
And hearing the foul mouthed repertoire
From the kitchen of the cook.

It would seem a lovely evening
Filled with cowboy merriment, but
Enjoyment from this ritual was not what we derived.
See, none of us wanted to be there,
Rather in our tents, but we had to wait 'til sundown
Or in there we'd broil alive.

On the outside acting saddened,
But smiling from within
We'd amble to our teepees when the temperature was right
Dog-tired
Muscles aching from the day's ten hour ride,
We'd burn the ticks out of our legs
And drift off for the night.

Continued . . .

The slam of an egg-filled frying pan
Would wake us from near death,
The wrangler would unsaddle,
We'd stumble to the shack
To scarf our food like animals, no time to take a breath,
Then out to catch the horses
And race to cinch your kack.

Camp coffee gets cold fast
When it's drunk at three a.m.
It gets down in your stomach and it starts to turn to ice
You feel as though it will surely come creeping up again
And you may complain about it once,
But you'll never do it twice.

'Cause sniveling isn't something taken kindly by this lot
You're apt to get a razzin' that could last you near a week
You grit your teeth
And bear it
Thank God for what you got
Remembering that predators wait to feed upon the meek.

The temperature hits ninety
My throat gets hot and dry
Cows are getting squirrely, hard to keep them all in line
Jim looks back across the valley
Sees the one that I passed by,
And begins to get "that look"
As prickles move up my spine.

No one but me could understand the reason for his words
If I told you what he said
Your impression would be wrong.
They were like sharpened daggers as vicious as I've heard,
But they were laced with good intentions
And I knew it all along.

Still they were so hard to handle
As they cut down to the core
He'd get right down to yelling
He could go on for a mile.
I never expected favors, hard work and nothing more
Sometimes though I wished like heck
That just once he'd crack a smile.

The boys are getting moody
We go through this every day
They need someone to blame it on
And I'm the greenhorn kid
Pat always had a mean streak
That came out in strange ways,
And we couldn't please him either,
No matter what we did.

Still, somehow,
We always managed to try to work together
Though I must admit at times
Murder must have crossed my mind.
When the work was done that evening,
Things would all get better
We'd sit there in the shade
And play rummy to unwind.

See, it's just another day
Nothing special, nothing new,
It would be the same on any ranch, I think,
I just tried to keep on doing all the things I had to do,
And reached up for a firm hold
So I wouldn't start to sink.

Now gazing through the heat waves
That slither through the air
I can see a yellow pickup
Kicking dust and riding high.

It's time that I got back for school,
And I never thought I'd care
But looking through that rearview mirror,
I feel like I could cry.
'Cause it isn't what you couldn't do
Or what you didn't know
That really makes a difference
When it all comes to an end.
It's how hard you tried while you were failing,
And the lessons that helped you grow
That make you look back on one hellish summer,
And wish you were there again.

PASSING THE MANTLE

Vess Quinlan

How small he was
And how he struggled
With the work;
He irrigated, fed, doctored,
And learned, as I had,
The difference between
Right and close,
Then sought my approval
To validate his knowing.

How strange it seems,
And how right,
That a simple passage
Of time has brought
Us here where I finish
This day of favorite work
And look to my son
For his approval.

A COWBOY'S MORNING

Royce W. Hodge

As a gray light appears
The morning begins to gleam
The crackle and smell of a small camp fire
The rush of a nearby stream.

On the fire a pot of water boils
To brew that amber drink
Bacon's fryin' and eggs near done
A good time to ponder and think.

What a wonderous thing that God has done
Creating this beautiful land
From rugged mountains to tender meadows
A wilderness at hand.

This is a cowboy's morning
The beginning of a brand new day
A moment to take his hat off
And bow his head and say . . .
    Thank You Lord.

Artwork by Norm Deitchman

NORMAN
DEITCHMAN

OF HORSES AND MEN

Jay Snider

Some are blessed with tranquil passing
While others meet a tragic end
Truth is, it's never easy
When you've lost a trusted friend.

As horses go, it's sometimes told
In simple words that cowboys use
He dern sure was a good one
He's the kind you hate to lose.

He's the kind you'd ride the river with
Roam the canyons and the breaks
In rough country and wild cattle
He'd be the one you'd take.

His efforts weren't ruled by stature
With him you'd finish what you'd start
His limits were governed only
By the dimensions of his heart.

His expectations were simple
Merely fairness from a friend
But when he'd feel the need to run
Don't try to fence him in.

Pure poetry in motion
As across the plains he'd fly
A tried and true compadre
In a seasoned cowboy's eye.

His courage was unmatched by mortal men
From conquistadores to kings
Cowboys sing his praises
At roundups in the spring.

Continued . . .

125

Ain't it strange how thoughts of horses lost
Mirror those of men passed on
And thought they've gone to glory
Their spirit's never gone.

Sometimes simple words seem best
When final words we choose
He dern sure was a good one
He's the kind you hate to lose.

THEM COWS

I ain't too well educated
Haven't spent much school room time
So I ain't too good at making up
Those fancy cowboy rhymes.

Someone said "Body language."
Is one good way of telling things
But I don't have the time for that
Besides, I don't know what it means.

But I do have one advantage
When I've worked up a little steam
You'll be safe a' bettin' moncy
That them dang cows know what I mean!

ONE SERAPHIC RIDE

Buck Ramsey

As dark was spreading on the air
Old Dunder came in grinning
Like some lit candled pumpkin face,
And well before they'd cleaned their plates
He loosed a yarn he didn't care
Would keep them up unspinning.

And sure enough the tale he told
Kept even Kid from nodding,
For it bought back a dear old friend
Who played him out another end
From when his last they laid him cold
And deep in prairie sodding.

As Dunder prowled along the rim
Where Dog Creek cuts a canyon
He reined up at the cliff edge where
Old H's horse took to the air
And crashed to earth and rendered him
The seraphim's companion.

He heard his name from pretty close,
And there was H astride
A Roman nosed strawberry roan
(Old Dunder guessed he was the one
The song said was the only hoss
The twister couldn't ride).

Old Dunder said he sauntered out
To see if he was seeing
What his eyes told him he saw
And it was H, the old outlaw,
Of that there was no room for doubt,
So he came close to fleeing.

But H let loose a seraph's laugh
And slapped a leather thigh,
And wound his hat round in the air

128

Till Dunder shook aside the scare
And joined this part at least by half
Back from his home on high.

"We'uz sittin' 'round," he said H said,
"And augerin' Charlie Russell
To string again old Brewster's ride
When he pitched off that high cliffside,
And though they knew that he was dead,
He hadn't pulled a muscle.

"Well, Charlie heads the cowpunch crowd
Where our tribe keeps its camp,
And when he sees you prowlin' here
He sends me joggin' to appear
And take that ride, but this time proud,
That snuffed out my life's lamp."

And then this cowboy seraphim
On Hell's worst unbroke stuff
Right easy one-hand rolled a smoke
And chuckled like he'd thought a joke
And struck a match to suck him in
A large old earthy puff.

Well, he would have to wait a bit,
For Roany kicked the lid off,
Turned loose to show what he was worth–
He stormed the air and shook the earth–
But it was clear no wall-eyed fit
Would make H be got rid of.

The sulphur smell that filled the air
When H's match was burning
As best old Dunder knew to tell,
Reminded his old horse of Hell,
So now he pitched for Heaven's fare,
If fare there was for earning.

He blasted up to paw a cloud
And wrinkled up his spine
And sunned his belly and both sides

Continued . . .

129

And busted sod with fencerow strides—
Old Dunder said, "He pitched it proud.
That beast was plumb sublime."

But H hanged tough, rocked with a grin,
Stayed like a camel's hump.
So then the roan in desperation
Set out to end this altercation
And bucked straight for the canyon rim
To take his final jump.

Old Dunder said it seemed unfair
For H to try again
To make it through the same old ride
That was his last before he died;
To undo what is done is rare,
To try is mostly vain.

He sadly rode up to the rim
To see the scene again
He'd seen the day H crashed and died,
But when he looked out o'er the side
He saw a sight that ticked him
More than a four inch rain.

Old Roan sprawled in a cottonwood—
It was the dam'dest sight—
Old H, still fast there in the saddle,
Asked, "Say old pard, did I hang and rattle?
But this match blew out, so if you could,
Would you spare a man a light?"

When Dunder's yarn was all unstrung
It must have been eleven,
But he'd not let them go to bed
Before he raised a hand and said,
"I say we vote it four to none,
The roan ends up in Heaven."

THE LAST GATHER

Rusty McCall

It's gonna be a long sad day,
They had to sell the ranch,
And we're selling the horses today.

That appy over there sure could buck,
You best know how to hang on,
Or be friends with lady luck.

The palomino was rough to ride,
I didn't much care for him,
He'd make you hurt inside.

The sorrel was one of the best,
I'd take him anywhere,
He'd pass my every test.

Big or little, short or tall,
Tough or tame,
God, I'm gonna miss 'em all.

I reckon I'll be movin' on,
I loved them horses,
Now they're gone.

It's time to move on anyways
'Cause my war bag's packed,
And I'm leavin' today.

LIFE I CHOSE

Glenn Moreland

As I gather the ponies in the dawn,
I wait for the sun which is too long.
My chilled bones are trembling with my soul
And I'm wondering how it could be so cold.

I watch the rising of the sun.
Like molten lava, it creeps over the rim.
Yet it fails to warm my bones
But my soul is revived once again.

As I ride through the day the sun is on high
And I long for the coolness of the morn.
I wonder how it could have been so cold
When now it has gotten so warm.

As I push the ponies down the trail
I wonder at the life I chose.
With the creak of my saddle I ride along
And now the dust begins to blow.

I could have had a city job
With all the comforts of a home,
But I know I would not have been happy
When I got the urge to roam.

So now I'm trailing horses,
My soul is at ease,
And I am thankful to the Lord.
I can do as I please.

QUAKIE BRAILLE

Bimbo Cheney

Did you ever get that feeling
      like you were in a special place,
Where not too many folks had been,
      and where the spirits touched your face?
And you feel that there's a reason,
      but you can't quite pin it down,
That you were picked to be there
      when there was no one else around.
I don't know why I was chosen,
      but that happened once to me,
When I was riding in the mountains,
      weaving through the quakie trees.

We had some steers on forest permits
      and the lease was running short,
So the boss sent me to fetch 'em,
      so as to keep him out of court.
Now, I had been up on that mountain
      probably twenty times, or more,
But I'd never been up quite that high,
      I hadn't been on that trail before,
When I come across some carvings
      on a tree there by the trail.
Two names were carved inside a heart,
      in lasting quakie braille.

Continued . . .

Now, that alone weren't special—
     I had seen carvings many times—
But I think these were the oldest,
     carved in 1889.
As I set my horse and watched 'em,
     two small figures caught my eye
In the underbrush behind 'em,
     and I ceased to wonder why.
These figures, too, had carvings,
     and they matched those on the tree.
Time hadn't been so good to them,
     but they sure matched I could see.

The names carved on that quakie
     were "Cy" and "Anna Fay."
Those same names on wooden markers
     crowned two forest-guarded graves.
My imagination took control
     and I was back in '89,
And I saw Cy with his folding knife
     pledge that their lives would entwine.
And then I saw them riding
     on that same trail I had rode,
Stopping many times thereafter,
     in that shade there by the road.

And not just when they was courtin',
     but many times besides,
And I think it was their special place
     till the day I made that ride.
At first, I thought to pull some weeds
     and knock down all that brush,
But then I thought the better,
     why disturb them with my fuss?
So I straightened up the markers,
     piled some stones back upon the mounds,
Put some flowers in-between the sweethearts,
     forked my horse, and rode back down.

Since then I have kept their secret,
       I haven't told one soul till now,
For some fifty years they have slept up there,
       where the two first made their vows.
Time will not erase it,
       it's engraved like quakie braille,
What I saw there on that mountain
       and those sweethearts' secret trail.
I suppose in time they'll vanish,
       the marks on those boards and the tree,
But never will they vanish from this cowboy's memory.

So, I wrote it down on paper,
       hopin' these words would last,
Can then preserve their story
       that I tell here from the past.
I hope you folks will tell your children,
       and they will then tell theirs,
About that heart that's carved on that quakie
       and those folks that rest up there.
And maybe when you are asked
       what love is by some youngster at your knee,
You will tell them of that special place
       that once was shared with me.

Artwork by Norm Deitchmann

The Women: Neighboing Poets

Antique Photo   Courtesy Beth Coad & Family

GATES

Barbara Hall

One of the stories I've heard all my life
Is about why a rancher takes a wife
So here's the facts that everyone knows
Everywhere he drives, everywhere he goes
There's a good many gates to open and close
Who gets the task? Why . . . the lady he chose!

Generally speakin' it's not much of a chore
She jumps out of the pickup and slams the door
Darts to the gate and grabs the gate stick
A gentle pull and the gate's down real slick
But sometimes there's mud slick as snot
Or snow to her knees or it's just plain hot.

Then there's the gate that's way too tight
She pulls and strains with all her might
With some good advice from the helpful guy
Sittin' in the pickup watchin' her try
"Dammit, hon, push on the top," he'll surely yell
Or "You got to push the bottom down, gal."

Some gates are awkward and heavy to handle
Some gates are built of wire made to tangle
They come down real easy and drag off the road
But getting them back up is an art to behold
She separates the bottom wire from the second from the top
But then the second from the bottom grabs on to the top.

You get the picture, so I guess I can ask,
Would you expect a rancher to do this task?
Now I've explained what I've known all my life
There's one main reason why a rancher takes a wife.

FIRST SADDLE

Kay Kelley

There's a special thrilling moment
Felt when you've got colts to break,
That makes the hard work all worthwhile,
And those chances that you take.

It happens when you step up on
Them for that very first ride.
You don't know if they'll fall apart
Or just take it all in stride.

Nice ones us'ally remember
Those hours you spent on the ground,
The sacking, hobbling and driving—
Teaching them to turn around.

For them it's just a matter of
Adjusting to packing you,
'Cause you've laid a firm foundation
Of teaching them what to do.

Then there's those snaky, broncy colts
That before their schooling's done,
Even with the blindfold on try
To "reach out and touch someone."

Their kind's more unpredictable.
They're more likely to explode.
You'd better be a fork-ed hand,
If you're going to get them rode.

This maiden voyage is kinda like
Exploring a last frontier,
A cowboy's footsteps on the moon,
Where eagerness covers fear.

So, it is a true adventure
Right there in the breaking pen,
When you're sitting in that one spot
Where no one has ever been.

GRANDMA'S ROSES

Jane Morton

The men cut grandma's roses down.
     They said they blocked the view.
Where driveway met the county road, a mishap might ensue.

And then they sprayed the roots and ground,
     so plants could not re-grow.
It was the Harison's yellow rose she'd planted long ago.

They could have left the bushes there
     and cut them back a bit.
Had Grandma been alive that day, she would have had a fit.

I wasn't there when it was done or would have stayed
     their hand.
At least I could have saved some shoots
     had I known what they planned.

I guess they didn't know that rose had come by wagon train.
Well-wrapped in dampened gunny sacks,
     it crossed the western plain.

Gram painted blooms on chinaware and won a state fair prize.
Those flowers kept on blooming even after their demise.

Those roses were our heritage as much as was the land.
It didn't matter to the men. They didn't understand.

Though antique roses could be bought,
     they wouldn't work for me.
They wouldn't be my heritage or speak my history.

Continued . . .

Dad said you couldn't kill the things.
        I thought that he was wrong.
I knew that little rose was tough, but probably not that strong.

Those plants withstood the wind and cold,
        the hail and searing heat.
But in the face of this attack, they went down to defeat.

The sight of roses dying there had torn me up inside.
I felt as wasted as the leaves, on canes they'd tossed aside.

For when they sprayed the roses' roots,
        they got some of my own.
A part of me died back that day.
        My heart weighed many stone.

Come spring I saw a little shoot the far side of the fence.
The Harison's rose was coming back, and here was evidence.

I've come to think my family was something like that rose,
A tough and prickly people who had weathered many blows.

They generally weren't people who could give in graciously,
But struggled through hard times and debt
        and clung tenaciously.

And when they seemed most down and out,
        and all their hope near gone,
By drawing strength from land they loved,
        together they hung on.

DON'T ASK ME

Peggy Godfrey

How do you know when a calf will be born?
What time do ya come in the house?
What do ya do when your truck breaks down?
Do the coyotes mess with your cows?

When do ya have the last killing frost?
How much rain in a regular year?
How many cows can ya run on an acre?
Can ya tell if you're in the right gear?

How can ya tell the time by the sun?
What time do ya usually eat?
What can I do to help you out?
How can you EAT them for meat?

How much wood do ya need for winter?
Do ya have to be "good" to get hired?
Can ya tell if your truck is gonna get stuck?
Hey, don't ya ever get tired?

Have you ever thought about moving?
What do you do all day?
What do you do when you need stuff?
Walmart is HOW FAR AWAY???

How can you stand not going to town?
What things about town do you miss?
What do you do when the weather is bad?
Aren't ya scared living out here like this?

You go ask these questions to new folks
They'll probably think them amusing
'Cuz the longer you're here, the harder it gets
Experience is so darn confusing!

MY HANDS

Frances May Dorr Wheeler

I look at my hands, all gnarled and rough
And think of the things they have done,
All of the ways they have served me
In snow or in cold, in dust and in sun.

They have fingered the strings of a violin,
They have held staples and stretched wire,
They have cuddled a downy chick with care,
And pulled the calf from the mire.

They have tenderly cradled a newborn babe,
And smoothed the brow of the dying.
They have clapped with pleasure at fun times
And comforted those that were crying.

So I try to appreciate my misshapen hands
That have worked so hard through the years
And remember the feel of the special touch
Instead of the pain that brings tears.

DINING OUT

Yvonne Hollenbeck

When you live out in the country, it's really quite a treat
When, maybe once of twice a year, you might go out to eat.

It happened once last summer after helping put up hay,
My husband asked if I would like to eat in town that day.

Well, I was quick to answer "Yes," then hurried to prepare;
I changed into my best old dress and fixed my windblown hair.

In nothing flat, our pickup truck was headed down the lane;
A dinner date with hubby was like lighting an old flame!

I'm visualizing candlelight as music softly plays,
Imagining the kindly things to me he just might say!

And as the pickup bounced along, I dreamed of even more;
When at the edge of town we pulled up to the old feed store.

I told him I would wait outside while he picked up some feed,
Cuz the guy that usually waits on him don't have a lot of speed.

Besides my shoes were killing me, I thought I'd rest my feet.
He said, "You'd better come on in, if you would like to eat."

Then pointed to a banner on the door that I could read
For the annual pancake supper at the local Feed & Seed!

But next week is his birthday and instead of grilling steaks,
I'll just invite his buddies out and fix 'em all pancakes!

WHEN I LEAVE THIS LIFE

Elizabeth Ebert

When I leave this life as we all must do
And the prairie I've loved through the long, long years,
There's a single boon that I ask of you:
Don't waste one precious day in tears.

Have a funeral if you feel you must
With the usual rituals for the dead,
A plain pine box, not satin lined,
But with blanket, preferable in red.

No cloying masses of hothouse flowers,
Just a cluster of bright balloons, and then
No extolling those virtues I never had,
Just a simple prayer and a soft "A-men."

Let the memories be of the happy times
Let the sound of laughter grace the day,
Find an old cowhand with an old guitar
To yodel me joyfully on my way.

And later, whenever the time seems right,
On a sunny day from a greening hill,
Scatter my ashes into the wind,
Then I shall be part of the prairie still.

SHOULDN'T WE GO TO THE HOUSE FOR A HORSE?

Echo Roy Klaproth

When it comes to the two-legged species of man
and the variance in language that we speak,
it's a wonder we ever get anything done
or stay together for longer than a week.

An example that readily comes to mind—
workin' livestock and dealin' with the same—
was doctorin' a sickly yearlin' heifer
we found one spring mornin' in the rain.

Immediately our minds both went to work,
two diff'rent directions with no hope for recourse;
him statin', "You drive and I'll rope 'er right here,"
me askin', "Shouldn't we go to the house for a horse?"

He took that like a slam to the midriff, you know,
masculinity threatened, his impatience foretold
the pace of the day when he charmingly said,
"This'll work if you simply do what you're told."

The hairs on the nape of my neck stood up,
which blocked all reason and hearing as well,
so I barely remembered the rest of the plan
as I fired up ole blue and circled pell-mell.

"Line 'er out, line 'er out!" he directed from the back,
so I tried, bein' careful not to make a mistake,
but just as he threw, that heifer ducked right,
and seein' he'd missed, I stepped on the brake.

He gathered up quickly in a scary like calm
pointin' and indicatin' we'd try it again,
so I drove on real slowly to separate her,
but this was a deal that I couldn't win.

Continued . . .

"Can't you go any faster, we don't have all day!"
so I gave it some gas—with no analysis . . .
but my rearview mirror told the story quite plain
'cause he was standin' in the pasture—like this . . .

It was about that time the dog left the scene,
tail tucked as he scattered up over the hill,
and if I had any sense I'd have followed along,
but now 'twas a matter of will against will.

"Do you think we can do this, time's wastin' you know?"
and I thought, "You bet, buddy, just swing yer rope,"
as I once again sorted our girl from the herd
then straightened her out in a nice, easy lope.

And things looked like they'd work, at least from my view,
she was headed okay as he made his pitch.
I silently prayed, watchin' action unfold
when suddenly, abruptly, we crossed a ditch.

Now the language exchanged can't ever be shared
and it's needless to say we were both some shook up,
but there's no accountin' for stubborn when mad
and as to who was winner at this point—a toss up.

One advantage, the heifer was slowin' down some,
remember she was ailin' and in need of our help,
but despite her tongue waggin' she found second wind
just as the next launch crossed over her scalp.

That's when we should have just quit and gone home
but pride was established and had now reached its peak,
and who coulda' guessed with those wide open miles
that today'd be the day I'd drive into the creek.

Three hours later with the heifer still free
the two of us walked in discordant discourse;
he cussed my drivin', the rope, the rain, and the cow,
and by now I was whinin', "If we'd gone for a horse . . ."

BORN TO BE A COWBOY

Sam DeLeeuw

A weathered drawn and hardened soul
There's poetry upon his face
Deep lines that map a rugged life
That was never commonplace.

He was born to be a cowboy
To ride upon this sun soaked land.
To make his way throughout his life
With a hard and calloused hand.

He was born to be a cowboy
And it's hard for him to change
To watch selfish greed, like fences,
Takin' away the open range.

His reddened eyes recite the woes
They've encountered those bygone years.
A heart not nearly healed nor whole
Feels all those miles of aches and tears.

His eyes search out the dust beyond
He stands alone amidst the change
His fading way of life draws close,
Much like the disappearing range.

A broken heart, like broken bones,
After a fall, takes time to heal.
To once again git up, stand tall,
And the sharp pains of change conceal.

The poetry etched upon his face
Leathered, cragged and solemn bound
Recites the loss of life and soul
That may never again be found.

Continued . . .

When things in life are taken away,
Oft' times they are never replaced.
The cowboy and his way of life
Some say, could shortly be erased.

He was born to be a cowboy,
But, he will never be replaced
The cowboy life out in the West
Will never die or be erased.

I LIVE IN A ZOO

Charlotte Thompson

I'd say if you're 'gonna have children
I've got money to cover all bets
That if you're gonna' have children
They're gonna' wanna' have pets.

At first it didn't much matter
I'd try to go light on the boys
'Cuz Lord knows we didn't have money
To buy them all fancy toys.

And a couple horn toads and lizards
In some sand in an old gallon jar
How could I ever expected
Things would get out of hand quite this far?

One cold winter morning the kids
Had all gone out with their dad
A neighbor came over to visit
About the first company I'd had

Well, I boiled us both up some water
And we sat down with our tea
When a cottontail hopped through the kitchen
Right by this neighbor and me.

That neighbor, she got kind of nervous
As the cottontail hopped down the hall
She finished her tea, left suddenly,
Never has come back to call

And once my best friend had come over
On the couch she was going to retire
Suddenly she started screaming
I thought the place must have caught fire!

I grabbed for my robe and ran quickly
To see what had upset my poor guest
Slade had forgotten his box turtle
You can imagine the rest!

Continued . . .

For a long time they had a pet curlew
A bird with long legs and neck
When I asked how they had caught it
They looked like I was dumber than heck

Why, of course, T.J. had just roped it
Or it kind of just ran in his loop
So he jerked up his slack, flipped it on its back
The horse trailer made a good coop.

Once Slade brought in a grasshopper
Tied to a horn toad with a string
He sat them on the floor, and the horn toad ran off
Draggin' that poor little thing

I yelled, "Slade, you're sadistic!
I want those animals outside and both freed."
He shrugged and pouted, "Sadistic?
I was just breaking that hopper to lead."

That summer they had grasshopper rodeos
I'm sure you never heard of such a thing
They'd cut out cowboys of paper
And tie them on grasshoppers with string

Then they'd set on the ground in a circle
And let hoppers go by one by one
In a loud voice they'd announce, "That's Nik Thompson
On a hopper named Son-of-a-gun."

They caught Whistle Pigs in Montana
And once Wendy even got bit
I was sure she was gonna' get rabies
So I threw a big hairy fit.

The kids are all grown up now
And the empty nest syndrome is true
But I can't say for sure which is better
The empty nest or living in a zoo.

ARIZONA HERITAGE

Nona Kelley Carver

When I ride along on the Mogollon,
Where the ponderosa pines grow tall,
There's a coolness in the morning breeze
In the glory of the fall.

When the little aspens color up
With their trembling leaves of gold,
Then I think again of our heritage
And recall the days of old.

When the west was new and the cattle grazed
On the ranges wild and free,
And our grandparents sought for a better life
To pass on to you and me.

They rode these canyons and these hills
While the sunset colors blazed,
And knew each inch of the mountain grass
Where their herds of cattle grazed.

Some paid their debts with their life's own blood
As they worked to settle this land.
Some were successful, some were not,
But their courage was bold and grand.

They rode these trails when the winter snows
Lay in drifts all white and steep,
And in summer time when the burning sun
Followed them into canyons deep.

Now we journey on and recall in song
Their memories and their dreams.
And we'll not let go of the things we know,
'Though Father Time has his schemes.

Let's take a moment to reflect
And recall in memory.
And appreciate the heritage
That they gave to you and me.

GRANDMA'S PULLIN' UP DRAG

Sue Jones

I've heard it said that the West is dead,
But partner, I hate to brag:
Small saddles with big dreams made a handsome team
With Grandma pullin' up drag.

Cowboy kids love the land, and understand
When hearts are brave and true;
And the smallest of all will push, scrap, or crawl
To be part of Grandpa's crew.

One slipped a cinch, got dumped, didn't flinch;
Another just had a loose girth.
But the oldest can track and sure bring 'em back,
Showin' how much she's worth.

With hat, spurs, and vest, he's ready for the quest;
The youngest sits ready to roll;
He and his cousins are watching as dozens
Of cows bawl at the waterhole.

Grandmas always worry and tend to hurry
While bringin' up the rear.
Keepin' an eye on the little guys
Who are completely absent from fear.

After all, it wasn't so long ago, though,
That Grandma rode the same seat;
Ridin' bareback gatherin', and takin' chances in the lightning;
The challenge was pretty sweet.

Ranch kids today preserve yesterday:
They love this land, their cows, the flag.
They've got the best of the young ranching West
And Grandma pullin' up drag.

LOOKIN' FOR COWS, FAWN CREEK, 1993

Virginia Bennett

Oh, my surprised lungs catch for a breath . . .
Tho' my eyes keep starin' on down the road.
Was it you, with mystified and cursed intention,
That caused my heart to nearly explode?

Or was it your horse, that renegade bay,
The one with an eye purely demonic?
Did he side-pass right to avoid a sharp rock,
And make my spirit sing something symphonic?

Or was it my mare, 'cause she *is* in heat,
And she's been looking all day at that bay?
She's a flirty ol' hussy, and I wouldn't put it past 'er
To swing that big butt over your way.

It couldn't have been *me*, tho, I guess it *is* true
That my right spur was embedded in 'er side.
And I know full well, I trained 'er to leg cues
Back when I broke 'er to ride.

It coulda been the moon, I hear it's been waxin'
And there's just no accountin' for nature.
Them hosses know better, but they're plumb confused
When it's the moon manning their legislature.

And, now a cowboy don't really know it . . .
He's about as perceptive as a blind porcupine.
But when he's calculatin' some on where the cows are
That ol' moon can sure put a knot in 'is twine.

So, it might just have been the hosses' fault
And it might'a been some birds on the wing.
It could'a been the hint of sage on the air,
'Cause I know a gal won't fall for sech a thing.

Continued . . .

155

Hey, now, buster, we're workin' today!
There's no time for this, you scruffy ol' pard,
To be sparkin' or considerin' our options.
Heck, gettin' this job done with you is dang hard!

Yep, we been cowboyin' together for more'n twenty years
I count it somethin' so rare and so fine.
And I still get that shiver up and down my back
Whenever your stirrup rubs up against mine.

Artwork by Norm Deitchmann

156

THE HIRED HAND

Deanna McCall

We made a call to town
To have some help sent out,
The horses and us were wore out
I even walked like I had gout.

They said they'd send a gal out
She knew what ridin' was all about
We agreed it would be all right
And she'd arrive that night.

After supper I heard a truck come in
And went to check the bunkhouse again,
I was surprised to find her there
It did kinda give me a scare.

Well, she was experienced all right
And I was grateful for the poor light.
She looked so old and poor
Standing slumped in that old door.

Her battered hat had a hole in the crown
And strands of dirty hair hung down
Over a face lined with dust and crud
That water would have turned to mud.

There was a tattered scarf 'round her neck—
Her coat looked like she'd been in a wreck;
One sleeve was torn halfway loose
Where feathers floated in search of the goose.

Just as I was about to voice my doubt
I let out a strangled shout—
Recognition had come to me,
And I tried to gather some dignity.

For all my fears had come true
And there wasn't a thing I could do
But slam that bunkhouse door
And not look in that dam' mirror any more!

BACKROADS

Georgie Sicking

There is a place in Arizona,
Stays forever in my mind
Beneath lofty Mahon Mountain
Where a pack trail weaves and winds.

With Trout Creek turning, winding,
Beneath the mesas high,
Where the black hawk screams and circles
Beneath a bright blue sky.

The springs beneath the walnut tree
With water sweet and clear
We could hear the calling of the mountain quail
Watch the grazing of the deer.

Watch a mother antelope
Chase a coyote from her fawn
Smell the wild rose in bloom
At the breaking of the dawn.

Could hear the braying of the pack string
In answer to my call
With the brays reverberating
Against the mountain wall.

Now, if I were to go back there
Changes and progress I might find
So I'll not go back, but keep it clean and bright
In the backroads of my mind.

PEARL HART

Lindy Simmons

Of the women of the west there are bold stories to impart
Have you heard about the famous bandit lady, Pearl Hart?

She ran away from Canada desiring to be free
And married a Rough Rider in eighteen ninety three.

He left her with two children. She did what she thought best
She gave them to her family and went out to the West.

Alone without resources, no way to earn a wage,
Pearl joined with Joseph Boot and robbed the Benson stage.

She dressed in men's rough clothing, prepared for the assault,
And stepped out as the stage appeared and brought it to a halt.

The men who rode the fated stage were robbed by Joseph Boot,
While Pearl kept her gun upon the men, prepared to shoot.

And then they let the travelers continue in the stage
While Pearl Hart and Joseph Boot rode out into the sage.

But fate would soon determine that they would lose their way
Out in the Superstitions they wandered several days.

There the sheriff found them asleep along the trail
And brought them into Florence where they were sent to jail.

Pearl's time in jail was short, and none can surely say
What became of Pearl Hart when she went on her way.

We know a play was written 'bout the little bandit lady
Some believe she went back East and lived to be near eighty.

Robberies were frequent, our historians attest,
But Pearl's was the very last stage rob'ry in the West.

UNFINISHED BUSINESS

Lyn Messersmith

While Mama lit the coal oil lamps
Dad and I pretended it was me
that pulled off his dusty boots.
I set them up straight as could be,
leaving the long roweled spurs
still attached. Traced the graceful
stitching of green, blue, and red,
stepped in, teetered on underslung heels,
and as always, hopefully said,

"Next time let's order the ones
with yellow stars and butterflies."
"They cost too much. These wear better."
An answer we both had memorized.
Teasing now . . . "Who'd see 'em anyhow,
Only dudes tuck pant legs in."
I sighed; turned a dog-eared page
in the Blucher catalog, and
pointed out my favorites, once again.

Then clomped around the kitchen
To the tune of frying taters;
twisted an ankle, finally fell
down in a jingling tangle,
scrambling, amid Ma's orders
to please go fetch the broom
and quit tracking up her floor.
Dad growled, "What the hell?
It's gold dust, nothing more."

I never quite grew into the boots.
I've frequently fallen behind
attempting to follow his tracks,
livin' out Dad's dreams, and mine.
Didn't own custom built Bluchers,
just other brands, with names long forgot.
Pitched about a ton of gold dust.
Blucher's out of business now.
That seems odd, though.
We're not.

DADDY'S PARD

Jan Choate-Richins

He was just a little feller
Almost turning three,
When his dad says to him one night,
"Hey, Pard, come check heifers with me."

It didn't take him long to find
His boots and coat and hat.
And then he drove the pickup
While sittin' on Daddy's lap.

Now, Dad had checked those little sukeys
Just about two hours before,
And he hadn't expected to find a thing
When he opened that barn door.

It was a cold Montana night,
About 20 below!
So the heaters in that calvin' barn
Had a nice warm welcome glow.

Daddy was a packin' his little Pard,
Steppin' it off fast as could be,
When at the back of the barn,
A busy heifer he did see.

Oh, she was a tryin' real hard
To get the job done!
But Dad knew at a glance—
She was in for a hard run.

So he sat his little Pard down
And hurried out to the truck—
To get a rope, some calvin' chains
And pray for a little luck.

Well, time stood still
In the calvin' barn that night.
And the little Pard held on to that fence
With all his strength and might.

But at last the gory job
Was over— finished— and done.
And the little ol' mama cow
Proudly licked her baby son.

Dad squatted down
And rubbed his little boy's hair.
He said, "Well Pard, I didn't think
She had a prayer."

The Pard's eyes shot fire
And his emotions showed cold and bare!
He stomped his little booted foot and said,
"DAD, WHO PUT HIM IN THERE?"

TIME AND AGE

Jerry Brooks

With time and age
I've learned from the pitfalls
And the prattles.

When young,
I would scorn those called "snitches"
Then, or "tattles."

But any more,
While I might not thank God
For the snake,
I will bless Him
For the rattles.

INDEX

167

TITLE OF POEM	AUTHOR	PAGE
Them Cows	Kennington, Don	127
Thunderstorm	Trombi, Joette Conley	69
Time and Age	Brooks, Jerry	164
To Choose a Hero	Autrey, Leon	90
Tomboy	Strickland-Johnson, Dee	65
Unfinished Business	Messersmith, Lynn	160
Vets	Lindsey, Steve	17
Waitin' for Some Rain	Isaacs, Chris	16
Weanin' Time	Abbott, Neil	20
What Really Mattered	Chiantaretto, Lola	74
When Horses Talk War	Logan, Mike	98
When I Leave This Life	Ebert, Elizabeth	146
Where Do We Go From Here	Ellsworth, Phil	22
Wishin'	Moore, Ken	34
Words That Whisper . . .	Nelson, Joel	112
Zack	Dunham, Jim	14